GO AHEAD, JUMP!

THE LIFE STORY OF BILLY SCHNEIDER

JOANNE SCHNEIDER

GOSPEL FILMS™
PUBLICATIONS

©Gospel Films, Inc. Box 455; Muskegon, MI 49443-0455
616-773-3361 Toll Free: 1-800-253-0413 Fax: 616-777-1847 www.gospelcom.net

Gospel Films Publications, the publishing arm of Gospel Films, Inc. P.O. Box 455; Muskegon, MI 49443-0455 616-773-3361 1-800-253-0413 Fax: 616-777-1847

Visit us on the World Wide Web at http://www.gospelcom.net

ISBN 1-555-68-208-1

GFP Catalog #GFP0005
First Printing, September1997

Printed in the United States of America

Joanne Schneider
Phil 4:13

Becky Schneider
Phil 1:20

This book is dedicated to Sarah McCorkle.
God used your little hands to take down the first brick.

First and foremost, I thank God, without whose mercy Billy undoubtedly would be dead today.

Then, I want to thank Tom Mahairas for his persistence in sharing the Gospel, pursuing his childhood friend for seventeen years until that friend at last understood and accepted the good news.

Thanks, Mom Helen, for the special person you are to both Billy and me, as well as to many others. Thanks for sharing yourself with us, for allowing your life to be a part of Billy's story. We love you! Mom Evelyn, Dad John, Jimmy and Denise, thanks for sharing stories of your lives, for reliving memories, some of which are painful, for the sake of Billy's story.

Thanks, Thom, Ian, Sam, for believing that this book could be and for believing that I could write it.

Thanks, Bruce, for your expertise in editing and for your encouragement to this first time writer.

And Lorna Dobson, thanks for taking the time to critique and give direction.

To Gospel Films, especially to Billy Zeoli and J. R. Whitby, thanks for being friends, for the huge amounts of time spent with Billy and me, for pouring yourselves into our lives and into this project. And Zak, thanks for the beanie bears that stared at me while I hunched over the computer.

A special thanks to Harvey and Ereveene Gainey for their support and love throughout this project.

And Paul T., the "angelic" voice of GOTeL Ministries, your gentle spirit encouraged both of us through tough times (Beware, Paul, Schneitz says he's coming out of retirement!)

And to all our friends and families, without whose prayers and encouragement, your understanding of the demands of time, this book would still be just a dream.

Billy, thanks for your story. Thanks for digging into your past, even when it hurt, for being real in order that the Gospel might be effective. I know it was tough, but I also saw you grow through the experience of being transparent. And thanks for giving me time and space, for believing in me, for encouraging me in putting down word after word, and for your candid editing. I love you, dude. You know that, right?

– Joanne

The story of Billy Schneider is one of the most incredible stories you will ever read. I know that as you read his story you will enter into one of the supernatural evidences of the transforming power of the Gospel of Jesus Christ on our city streets. To see the transformation that has taken place in this man's life is to live through a modern day miracle.

I've known Billy since we were ten years old, and since he was ten Billy always stood out in the crowd. What I didn't know was what made him stand out - he hid and pushed all his hurt and pain down in his spirit. It came out as the class clown. Billy and I became close friends in Mr. Struggler's class, at Junior High School #52. Whether pitching quarters, getting drunk, getting high, or running around with girls, Billy Schneider and Tom Mahairas were inseparable.

When I first became a Christian in 1968, I began to pray that God would manifest himself to my friends. I thought, "Wow, if God could only change Billy!" Billy was the most impossible situation I could think of – a heroin addict, imprisoned, needy and lonely. All he needed was to know of the love of Jesus. As I began to pray that God would miraculously open Billy's eyes and save him, I watched Jesus go after Billy. You will see the sovereignty of God at work in the life of a street kid as you read *Go Ahead, Jump!* Your imagination will be activated with excitement as you see the transforming power of God in the life of Billy the Abused Child, Billy Words the Poet, Billy the Addict, Billy the Con, Billy the Child of God, and Billy the Evangelist!

Truly Billy's story needs to be heard throughout every city in America. The leaders in Washington need to take note of Billy's story. What the penal institutions couldn't do, what the drug rehabs couldn't do, what the mental institutions and half-way houses couldn't do, Jesus Christ and the power of His forgiveness could do!

I have watched Billy go from class clown, to a prisoner, to a cynical streetwise junkie, and then to an evangelist with heaven's wisdom on his lips. I have watched him struggle with heroin addiction, immorality, anger, fear, greed, loneliness, rejection, and HIV; and then, I watched Billy cast himself at the feet of Jesus and rise on the victory side.

With Billy Schneider, what you see is what you get, there is no pretense. He's quick to let you know what he thinks. With raw honesty he reveals his weaknesses and his faults. He is transparent and confrontational; he is not one to sweep things under the rug. Above all else, Billy is a sincere, genuine believer in every respect.

I've watched Billy now for more than ten years live in the reality of a free and forgiven life. I've watched him use his poetry and his ability with words to help people become free from drugs, free from drink, and free from depression. I've watched him struggle through his temptations, I've watched him go through testings, and I've watched him come through like gold, as a child of God. I've watched Gods loving discipline restore Billy, and I've watched him learn to be a man accountable to his church, his leaders, his friends, and his wife.

Billy Schneider is one of the most gifted communicators I have ever heard in my life. His message is not filled with Christian cliches, but with powerful, practical, pithy metaphors and quotes that you can hang your hat on. He hasn't been to the school of theology; he didn't receive his degrees from a seminary, but from the school of hard knocks and the penitentiary.

Billy doesn't seek for a position, but shares his passion for the lost. He truly is an evangelist to boys and girls, moms and dads, prisoners, drug addicts, business people, and everyone with whom he comes in contact. It's quickly obvious as he shares his story that the hand of God is on his life.

May God use this incredible true story for his glory. This is really what God is up to and doing through His Son, Jesus, in the lives of people in the inner city.

I could go on and on about Billy, but there are some things that I want to share from my heart. I still remember the day Billy called me up from Columbia Presbyterian Hospital to tell me, "Tom, you're the only friend I have that is still alive. Would you please come and see me?" I guess above everything that Billy has been, and is to me, he's my friend. I've never been around a guy who can be so upbeat and funny even while facing the most incredible circumstances and odds. When we were children pitching quarters, and my quarter was almost touching the wall, Billy would say, "Watch me, watch me land a leaner against the wall." You knew he was thinking about the odds and how hard it would be to land the leaner, but it sure wouldn't stop him from trying. That's Billy Schneider. I've watched my friend face HIV with incredible courage, trust, faith and hope. He tells young people all the time, "It's not that I'm HIV positive, it's that I'm HIM positive. It's not that I'm HIV positive, it's that I'm J-E-S-U-S positive." I guess that sums it up – Billy Schneider jumping with all of his problems, all of his hurts, all of his pain into the arms of Jesus.
"Go ahead, Billy, go ahead. Bill, go ahead, jump!"

May each of us learn to do the same.

– Tom Mahairas

Table of Contents

CONTENTS

Foreword

E DDERIC PATHETERIC

"Ask the animals, and they will teach you. . . ." (Job 12:7 NIV).

He came to us on a hot Sunday evening, an apparition in the shape of a dog, a nearly unrecognizable Chow. His hair was dirty, matted and thick, his stench unbearable.

He attracted my attention because he stood in the street, unmindful that he was impeding traffic. He moved slowly and aimlessly, with great difficulty.

"Billy! Look at this animal!" Billy came out to the street to see what I was talking about. He didn't have to stop and think about what to do. He just went right into the road to bring the dog to safety. There was a short chain attached to his filthy collar. Billy took the chain and led him off the street. We thought he might have been scrounging garbage cans for food, but a closer look suggested he likely did not have the energy to do even this.

What were we to do with him? He appeared old, looked sick, and was most certainly homeless. The situation looked hopeless. The humane thing would be to put this animal out of his misery. That certainly was our first thought. Of what value was he, anyway? But let's feed him first, okay? We gave him a pan of water and some dog food, and to our surprise he drank and ate all of it.

We searched the phone book for a local humane society or animal shelter. We found the number for an animal hospital, but could get no further than the answering service. We tried the police department, but they had no one who could pick up the dog until morning. Belton, South Carolina, was not well equipped for an emergency of this nature. And neither were we.

By this time it was dark. There wasn't much more we could do. Billy, with his tender heart, did not want to send the dog off to be destroyed, so we prayed that the beast would wander away so that someone else could deal with him.

When sleep came at last, both Billy and I had dreams about mangy dogs. In the morning we breathed a sigh of relief when we did not find him in our yard, each of us for different reasons: Billy could not bear to send him off on his final journey; I feared he might stay right where he was – in our yard. Frankly, I didn't want anything to do with him. We certainly didn't need another problem, another thing to take up our time.

I went off to work and nearly forgot about him. He was gone, his wretched hair out of ours. Thank you, Lord. At least we were kind to this creature of yours, weren't we? But as I drove home, the image of the forlorn dog returned to mind.

To my dismay, as I came into the driveway, who should slowly follow my car but The Creature!

"Oh, no!" I cried to Billy. "What will we do with this pathetic animal now?"

"It's ironic you should call him pathetic," Billy responded. "He was hanging out here and in the neighbor's yard when I got home this afternoon. I began calling him Edderic Patheteric. You know, 'Oh, Edderic Patheteric I am, I am...'" He sang a little ditty.

I couldn't help laughing. As much as I didn't want to deal with this creature, I knew that nothing happens to us by chance. Had he not been given life by God? Then we must respect this life. And are we not given dominion over the animals? If so, then we are responsible for the condition of those God places in our care. Had God directed him into our yard so that we could show him mercy? What a picture he was of our human condition before God. What mercy God has showed us! With that in mind, how could I say no when Billy insisted we do something to help improve this mutt's condition?

So Monday evening, we donned gloves, found scissors, and began snipping away at the thick matting. As the hair fell, the odor rose. But we persisted. Amazingly, Eddie, as we soon dubbed him, never resisted. We were able to remove only a tiny bit at a time, his fur was so thick and so caked with mud. "Eddie, if only you could talk!" I said to him. "How on earth did you end up in this dreadful shape?" We decided he must have been tied to his very short chain for a very long while. We had many questions that Eddie couldn't answer. So we just had to be content to help him, regardless of how he came to be this way. We thought of the abused people around us, who, like Eddie, may not be able to explain fully just how they came to be in their condition.

After an hour or two of hard work and a garbage bag half full of globs of gunk, we finally began to see a bit of skin. We tried an electric clipper, shaving a swath of bristly hair from his backbone. Now we could see he was little more than skin and bones, not the fat thing we earlier presumed him to be.

In the morning, I began calling for help. The local pet groomer didn't do Chows, explaining that they can be temperamental and vicious. We saw none of this in Eddie. Late in the day, we located a vet who would see him. Billy wrapped Eddie in a towel and he and a friend took Eddie in the car. As they sat waiting, who should walk in but a well-groomed lady with her well-groomed poodle, ribbons and all. The humor of the situation almost overtook Billy as everyone except Billy, Jerry and six-year-old Amber moved as far away as possible from pathetic, smelly Eddie. The vet pronounced Eddie about six years old, no fleas or parasites (not even a flea wanted to take up residence with Eddie!). He did, however, have heartworm and a severe infestation of ear mites. The doctor told us he was walking poorly because his extremely matted hair was cutting off circulation.

Well, with a $60 vet bill invested, it looked like Eddie was a keeper. We put him in the bathtub later that night, and Eddie just soaked quietly, his cute little face above water, looking like a baby seal. He protested nothing, allowing us to cut and brush and pull away at the mats. The water was red as the South Carolina clay when we were finished.

And, yes, he was cute! His curl of a tail began to wag a bit as we talked to him. He was now walking better, even trying to play basketball with the boys. The job was nowhere near finished, but Eddie was becoming more cheerful and content – like, well, a pet.

As I write this, Eddie is playing in the back yard, happy to be with us. He is beginning to bark – a muted, hoarse sort of bark. He looks a little strange with a bald spot on his back, and the rest of his hair now clipped short. But his trimmed tail bounces all over his back when he hears us. He and Billy are "bonding," with Billy pleased to receive "doggy kisses" from him. I'm a bit more wary of Eddie, but I offered him a bit of food the other day, which he took from my hand. I could feel his powerful Chow jaw on my finger, but he took care not to hurt me. We are building trust. In fact, I believe Eddie trusts me more than I trust him, and I feel a bit unworthy of that.

So, Edderic, you have taught us some valuable lessons. You have provided a great illustration with which to begin Billy's story. As others looked at Billy, many of them turned away like the poodle lady in the vet's office. It seems that the more groomed we become as Christians the more we tend to shun the smell and filth associated with "sinners." We fail to see that they have been chained by the devil himself. And don't we have the cure for their disease? To our shame, the lost of the world can seem more caring than some Christians. We might say that they have nothing to lose. But if we are Christians we have everything they could gain.

Some, like me, offer the excuse that we are just too busy to bother. An interruption is an annoyance rather than an opportunity. But what would we have missed had we followed my desire, or lack of it?

I found that I could avoid becoming smelly and filthy like Eddie by wearing gloves and showering. In order to clean Eddie, I did not have to become like him. I could go to him, touch him, wash him, yet not adopt his ways. It helps me understand that I can go into the world, armed with the cleansing water of the Word, and touch the human conditions caused by sin without falling into sin myself.

Others responded to Billy as the pet groomer did – keeping a distance from him for fear of his "bite." But just as Eddie responded to our touch with gratefulness and a wagging tail, so we may be surprised by the response of one with whom we may at first glance fear to share the gospel. Could it be that they would respond to a touch of love and kindness, just as Eddie has?

And just as Billy's heart responded to Edderic Patheteric – a bit of life created by God, and in this condition not by his own choice, should we not see beyond the sin, beyond the stink of the human condition, and into the reality that wherever there is life, no matter how wretched, there is hope? There is God, the creator of life. And doesn't He tell us that even our human goodness is filthy before Him? Of course we are not too clean to reach out.

As Eddie shows gratitude to us for taking him into our family, so also Billy feels a deep sense of thankfulness and gratitude to the person who saw beyond the exterior and into his soul, and who, over the years, "hounded" him with Jesus – the Jesus who, with one touch, can transform the lives of many from "Patheteric" to positive, from wretched to righteous.

Yes, Eddie offers a great opening for Billy's story. Billy does not mind being compared to him. The more one understands the wretchedness of his own human condition, the more one appreciates the great and mighty things God has done for him, and how He has had mercy on him. And as Eddie might cry if he could, "Why me?" so Billy cried "Why me?" many times in his life. Why am I being abused? Why am I such a mess? Why do I hurt so? Why does no one hear me? And later, Why me, Jesus? Why did you rescue me and change me and give me joy and reason to praise You daily? Yes, Lord, why me?

Billy's story is powerful. It is a story of deep pain, of great sin, of hopelessness, of incredible transformation, of tremendous joy and hope, of love and of humor. What Eddie cannot say, Billy can. It is a story of the amazing grace and mercy of Jesus Christ, whose love is deeper than the pain, greater than the sin. Billy's story is, after all, the story of Jesus Christ, who reached into the stench and filth of Billy's life to pull out a jewel of great beauty, priceless to Himself and now to many others.

CHAPTER 1

The George Washington Bridge

(Note: some names have been changed to protect identities.)

The view from the top may have been terrific, but Billy wasn't paying attention to the sunrise on the horizon, the water swirling below, or the amazing city spread out as far as the eye could see. He was instead focused on the snarled traffic, the police cars, and, especially, the beat cop who was climbing up after him.

Billy did not scale to the top of the George Washington Bridge for the view. His sights were set on something entirely different – he wanted to be heard. And for him, at that time, the only way he thought he could be heard was to be seen.

The date was March 11, 1977. For Billy, the dawn of this beautiful spring morning meant the end of a long night of shooting cocaine. Although his drug of choice was heroin, he had been using cocaine as well since the mid 1970s, often combining them. The effect of both together was called "speedballing." For the past five years, Billy had been on the Methadone program, a federally funded program in which heroin addicts could get their drug free of charge in synthetic form, called Methadone.

Although Billy was married, he and his wife Linda were separated, and he was living in a rooming house with a girl named Terri. Eventually Linda and Terri became good friends. The bond between them was Billy, and they both loved him. With the Hippie era still in full swing, people seemed to accept anything. "Peace" and "love" were words to live by in the 1960s and 1970s. "Everything is beautiful" and communal living were a part of the times.

There was a desperation about Billy. The world in which he lived seemed aimless. Reality and truth were sought in the panacea of drugs and "free love."

On this morning, Billy was up for talking. He was alone with Terri, but she was exhausted. "Please, Billy, get some sleep," she pleaded with him. Because of the cocaine in his system, he was not ready for sleep. Drumming through his mind was the need to be heard. But who was there to listen? Even his best friend Terri was sleeping, copping out on him. Feelings of desperation were overwhelming him. He thought of how cruel life was, and how frustrating.

Deep inside, Billy truly wanted to be free of drugs and welfare. Each time he was released from prison, he vowed to stay drug free. But each time, he was right back into the drug scene, usually within hours. The Methadone program was not freeing him from the bondage of drugs, as he had hoped. Rather, he was maintaining his habit with free drugs, and along with free drugs came free medical care and welfare. Billy's counselor at the Methadone program was compounding the problem by selling him cocaine. He was supplying it to Billy more cheaply than he could get it on the streets. He was no help. About three months earlier, Billy had been attacked at the program by a security guard. Billy felt the guard was a militant who did not like him. He had thrown Billy against a wall, and Billy had hit a radiator pipe and broken several ribs. He had been in pain for weeks, with ribs taped, sleeping on the floor and nursing a bitterness toward the guard. The government's way out for a heroin addict was no way out at all. It was just another trap.

Billy thought of his friends caught in similar situations, many of whom were minorities, Hispanic or African-American, and who could not speak for themselves in a way that would be heard. He felt compassion for them and wanted them to be helped as well.

Now out of cocaine, but his mind racing, he wrote several poems, one of them called "The Bridge," in an attempt to figure out what actually ties everything together. "I need someone to hear me, hear my poem, hear me cry!" he wept. Billy was bombarded by thoughts. Cocaine is a "why?" drug, opening the mind to questions for which there are no human answers. Billy began asking questions of God, but received no answer. Even God must be asleep, like Terri and everyone else. I've got to wake up God, he thought, and tell Him how messed up He is. With that thought, a plan began taking shape in his mind: if he climbed to the top of the George Washington Bridge, maybe he would be heard. Would God listen to him there?

The thought spurred him to action. He got up and dressed, walking out the door with his leather jacket and backwards baseball cap. Terri never woke up, which was unusual – she generally had a built-in antenna for Billy. It was 6:30 a.m. He wrote a note – who he was, what he was going through, his problems with the Methadone program, the trap it was, the cocaine, the security guard, ending with these words: "My friends are all trapped. Don't you hear me, God? My friends are all trapped. They're cattle on their way to slaughter. Let's find out who cares. I'll show you how much I care. People gotta listen! But how's that gonna happen? Everybody's asleep!"

With note in hand, he walked to the George Washington Bridge, about eight blocks away. Arriving at Fort Washington Avenue and 179th Street, he looked at the enormity of the bridge. He wasn't sure how he'd do it, but Billy Schneider was determined to make it to the pinnacle. He thought of climbing the expansion cables, but when he got close, he could see how huge they were and realized they were both too wide and too steep to safely scale. He couldn't make it this way.

He came to the Northeast Tower and decided this was the way to go. He would climb the crisscrossed metal girders. Just as he made this decision, he saw three boys approaching. He also saw a New York City police officer drive onto the bridge and position himself towards oncoming traffic, ready to direct in the morning rush hour. The officer was, of course, blissfully unaware of the twist his day soon would take.

Dropping the note, Billy began to climb, yelling to the boys as he started up, "Pick up the note and take it to the police!" It was a perfect setup. He would be immediately noticed, the note would be read. Someone would finally listen to him. The boys seemed terrified at first, not sure what Billy wanted, or if he might harm them. Then, realizing that something was out of the ordinary, and that Billy was not intent on hurting them, they caught something of the excitement of the moment. Billy could see that they understood what it was he wanted. He saw them pick up the note, handling it as though it were a letter bomb, and run with it to the officer, who was now standing beside his car. He saw the officer tear open the envelope, read the note, look up to see Billy, then jump into his car. He heard a siren begin to wail, slowing traffic. Now it was as though Billy were watching a movie, something outside himself, the drama unfolding before his eyes.

Soon Billy could hear sirens coming from all directions. As he continued to climb, he could see police cars coming from everywhere. It was the first time in his life that he could see the police coming. Before, they always had caught him by surprise.

For Billy there was no turning back. It was like a chess game for him. He simply would outsmart whoever might try to stop him until he was heard. Whatever he might have thought as he started from home toward the bridge, this was now serious business. He watched as the New Jersey police were notified and began converging. Traffic still moved, slowing as curiosity seekers stopped, looking up. Then, suddenly, traffic stopped completely. Why, Billy wondered? It was not until later that he understood that had he jumped or fallen, he could have caused serious injuries to totally innocent persons, and it was a responsibility of the police to avoid this if at all possible.

Billy heard the tower elevator start. It was a locked elevator, used only by the Port Authority. A few police officers began to climb up the tower the same way Billy was climbing. The first officer on the scene, the one who took the note, was the one who had first arrested Billy, back in 1965, for stealing a car. He also was the first to begin climbing after Billy. He had treated Billy shabbily in the past. Now he treated him like a kid.

"You freaking idiot, get down!" he roared. Billy was angry, but he was also completely in control, and determined to confuse Frank, the neighborhood beat cop. His experience as a roofer made it easy for him to shake Frank. Just by talking to Frank as he climbed, Billy made Frank look up at him, then down to the ground. Billy knew never to do that when climbing heights. Seeing that the trick was working gave Billy a sense of power, and he did something he now regrets. He urinated on Frank, yelling and swearing, "Get that ____ cop away from me!"

The sergeant on the ground, seeing Billy's agitation, ordered Frank off the bridge. "You're just riling him!" He knew that doing so could only increase the danger of the situation they all were facing. What Billy might do next could not be predicted.

After about 45 minutes of climbing, Billy arrived at the top of the bridge, 450 feet above the water. Just above him were the tower's red warning lights. He sat down on the highest girder. He heard someone in the elevator, just slightly below where he was sitting. They asked what Billy's religion was. "Catholic," he responded. He heard the elevator go down.

Billy sat alone on top of the bridge, thoughts and questions racing through his mind. Was someone going to return? Would they listen to him? Would they see to it that he got the help that he so desperately needed? He looked down at the water, wondering what actually happens to the body when it hits from such a height. Could he make a perfect dive and hit the water without making a splash, or would he twist and tumble and be driven away by the wind, smashing into the rocks below? As he looked down, police boats plied the waters, anticipating the jumper of a man they knew nothing about. Would he be just another leaper, driven to suicide through the snare of drugs, and later identified as William Charles Schneider, age 27, son of William Frederick Schneider and Helen Kern?

The crowd began to grow, onlookers below, people on rooftops, not wanting to miss the drama of the moment. Billy actually grew a bit bored sitting alone up on the bridge, looking out over the Palisades and the New York City skyline. As a bone for the crowd, he took off his baseball cap and sent it sailing. This was Billy Schneider's moment, time was essential, and he didn't want to lose the attention of the crowd. The cap fluttering down, who knew what might come next?

Twenty minutes later the elevator door opened again. Inside was a Catholic priest. He talked with Billy about his value, who he was, why he shouldn't jump. Finally Billy asked him, "Why have you never mentioned God?"

"Sometimes you don't have to mention God, but He's there."

"What do you mean by that?" Billy asked. The priest explained that he had been in his car on the way to a seminar, when the traffic stopped. Moments later he spotted a police officer and asked if he could be of some help. The officer replied, "You sure could. There's a guy up on the bridge who says he's Catholic." They agreed he might want the last rites before he jumped to his death. What they didn't understand is that Billy didn't want last rites, he wanted first rights – the right to freedom of speech, the right to be heard.

"Father, I don't want to jump! I want help. I'm trapped. I've got no peace. I'm tired of drugs." He told the priest of his frustration with heroin, with cocaine, with the Methadone program, of the need to be heard, of his friends who also were not being heard. He pleaded, "I'm not crazy! I don't need a psych ward. I need a different life!"

The priest promised he wouldn't let Billy be put in a mental institution. A rehab program in New Jersey was mentioned.

Billy agreed to come down only if the priest could get Terri to witness what the plan would be. "Who's Terri?" the priest asked. Billy explained and the priest agreed. Billy gave the clergyman her address, and again he was left alone at the top as the priest descended in the elevator.

Billy watched as the priest spoke with the policeman. He heard the sirens wail again, saw a police car cross the bridge into New Jersey, turn around, come back into New York. He saw every turn the car made on its route to the rooming house eight blocks away.

Later he learned they woke Terri up. She was absolutely frantic, thinking he must be dead. But no. Today, Billy was at the top of the George Washington Bridge.

Terry was brought up in the elevator, and she looked sadly at Billy, tears in her eyes. She felt so guilty for going to sleep at a time when he desperately needed her. Billy asked the priest to make promises to him in Terri's presence, which he did – absolutely no mental institution. "I'm not crazy," Billy said. "I just need help!"

The priest repeated his vow: "I won't let them put you in a mental institution. I'll see to it that you get help with your drug problem." At last, Billy placed his trust in the priest and worked his way down into the elevator.

In the elevator, however, Billy was immediately handcuffed, hands behind his back. Shackled, he was brought down before the crowd of onlookers, the police commissioner, news reporters, photographers.

He was placed into the back of the nearest police car along with Terri. In the front seat of the cruiser was Frank! The police commissioner leaned into the front window and said, "Frank, direct!" Once Billy was "safely" inside, his fate still unknown to him, the officials, reporters, police boats, and helicopters all began moving away. After five and one half hours, traffic began moving across the bridge. Life was back to New York's normal hustle and bustle.

Inside the police car, Frank, a "peon" as Billy called him, immediately began threatening and taunting Billy. "Wait 'til we get away from the crowd, you little_____!" And as soon as they were enroute and out of sight of the commissioner, Frank reached into the back of the car and grabbed Billy by the collar, jerking him up, and began slapping him in the face. Terri began to cry, "Please, don't hurt him!" At this, the car screeched to a halt and the driver, a sergeant, gave Frank a curt order. "Take your _____ hands off him! You hit him again and I'll shoot you!"

CHAPTER 2

The View from "the VUE"

Their destination was Bellevue Hospital. There was no drug rehab here! Billy knew in his heart where they were headed – to the psych ward. It was exactly what the priest had promised would not happen. Now Billy could weep "Why me? What was the use? Why try to be heard?" For all the good it did, he might as well have jumped.

On arrival they were met by more city police officials. Billy was hustled through a corridor filled with reporters seeking tidbits of information. He and Terri were separated at this point, with Billy brought into an office to await a psychiatrist, while Terri waited in the corridor, surrounded by police. At last the doctor arrived.

One of his first questions was whether Billy had ever been a patient at Bellevue.

"Oh, yes," Billy responded.

"Do you recall when that might have been?"

"Yes, Doc, I do. June 27, 1949, 2 p.m."

"What? You couldn't remember that far back! What were you admitted for?"

"I was born here that day."

The doctor continued questioning Billy, responding to Billy's story with "Uh huh . . . I see . . . Hmmm . . . I see . . . Uh huh." Billy and the doctor sized each other up quickly, the doctor thinking Billy was mentally unbalanced, and Billy feeling certain the doctor needed a checkup from the neck up. The doctor seemed to have no compassion or understanding. He was cold and clinical. His only recommendations were a shot of Thorazine, a frontal lobotomy or shock treatments, none of which was the answer to the immediate need that Billy felt. They were not a cure. They were only a means to control Billy. The doctor offered no real answers and seemed to show little interest in the problem.

"Why don't you consider climbing to the top of the George Washington Bridge insane?" he asked Billy.

Billy responded, "It is not insane. I am not insane. I just wanted someone to listen. Someone to hear. I wanted help." On and on the debate went, the doctor assuring Billy that someone would indeed listen to him in couple of days. He ended the discussion by shoving some papers across the desk to Billy, saying, "Here, you just sign these papers. I'll be right back." The doctor went into the corridor to assure the police that Billy was voluntarily signing himself into the mental hospital for seventy-two hours. Admission was complete. Another life had been saved from suicide. Backs patted. Good job.

Meanwhile, back in the office, Billy was saying to himself, "Isn't it funny, I never intended to jump. Ha! Ha! The joke's on them." Taking time to read the fine print regarding voluntarily admitting oneself to a New York State mental institution, Billy felt he still had an edge over the doctor. When the doctor returned to his office, he found a little blaze in his ashtray. Billy had torched the document he was asked to sign. The concept was crazy, not Billy! He was empty, lonely, hurting, crying out and still no one was listening. Not even God. But he was not crazy.

The doctor questioned Billy about what he had just done. Again Billy explained that there was nothing wrong with him mentally. He was not committing himself, despite what the doctor had told police and reporters. The news would be wrong. Billy did not recognize that the doctor held the upper hand. If this were a game of chess, Billy was in check. He now found himself being involuntarily admitted to a mental institution for an unknown period of time.

Billy was escorted to the sixth floor by an orderly, a nurse, two police officers, and Terri. Once on the sixth floor, the two officers were dismissed, the nurse opened a gate, and Terri left the elevator with Billy and the orderly. Terri was not allowed to enter beyond this point. She reached out her arms to hug Billy, tears pooling in her eyes. The nurse reacted by violently grabbing Terri and screaming, "You're not allowed beyond this point!" Angered at how the nurse treated Terri, Billy became frantic. He grabbed the nurse by her long hair and yanked her to the ground, warning her not to put her hands on Terri. The nurse yelled, screaming for orderlies, and blurting out other medical directions Billy did not understand. Four orderlies, one nurse and a hypodermic needle arrived, and Billy was just moments away from a massive dose of Thorazine. With that job accomplished by force at the gate and in front of Terri, "Nurse Ratchet" signed orders – NO VISITORS. TEND TO MAKE PATIENT VIOLENT. With the stroke of a pen, all Billy's visiting privileges were gone.

Terri was pulled away screaming, "Don't hurt him! Please! He's sorry!" As though anyone would listen to her either.

Billy arrived in the psych ward freshly drugged up, alone, unheard. No visits allowed. Remembering his time in prison, he realized he was now merely trapped in a different cell. The bars were the same, but the prisoners different. Their faces were empty, their minds devoid of thought, made so by drugs, shock therapy, or surgery. Their movements were mechanical. Psychiatric care in the 1970s was based on control, not compassion. Billy seemed doomed to end up a captive, as well.

What about the promises made by the priest while on the bridge? Obviously, the trip to the top had accomplished nothing. The bridge was just a view from the "Vue," as Billy gazed out a window. Newspapers later reported "Man Climbs Bridge In Plea for Help," but who really listened?

Within minutes, the Thorazine began to take effect. Although he had been on many drugs, the Thorazine, as Billy experienced it, "toasts you, makes you like a marshmallow." He could feel his thoughts, his body, his reflexes, slowing down.

Determined to not give in to the drug and drown in the psychiatric ooze of Thorazine, Billy began to walk around the unit to acquaint himself with his surroundings. It was something he had learned from his Uncle Sonny – "always case the place." He checked out the bathroom, the day room, the nurses' station, visiting rooms, and the sleeping quarters. He learned there were about fifteen other residents there. As he saw the Thorazine shuffle, the blank faces around him, he began to whisper to himself, "I'm going to be okay." It became a refrain he played again and again: "I'm going to be okay, I'm going to be okay. Three more days I'll see the Doc. Tick, tock, tick, tock. Three more days I'll see the Doc. I'm going to be okay, I'm going to be okay."

Three hours later, the phone rang, and one of the robot-like patients informed Billy that the call was for him. It was Terri, crying, concerned, compassionate. She assured him she was going to get him out. She would speak to the mayor and tell him Billy didn't belong in a mental institution. As they were speaking, something began to happen. Billy felt as though a hypodermic needle was stuck in his tongue, injecting air and blowing it up. He tried to tell Terri he would be okay, but his speech became slurred. He hung up and rushed to the nurses station in panic. He pointed to his tongue. The nurse understood immediately what was wrong; he was having a Thorazine reaction. She went to a cupboard, took out two little white pills, slipped them in a cup and gave them to Billy. He realized at that moment that he could read lips. In his panic he saw, rather than heard her say, "Take these pills and relax. Just relax. You're going to be okay." With no other options, he obeyed. He relaxed. In about fifteen minutes, he was back to normal (Thorazine-induced normal, that is) and continued inspecting his surroundings.

He sat down on a bench in order to introduce himself to his new drug friends. He was intrigued by a young black girl sitting near him, not because of her beauty or her speech, but because of what she was doing. She had large scabs over her whole body, which she was picking off and placing into her mouth. In his Thorazine-programmed state of mind, her disgusting behavior was fascinating.

Off in the distance he heard the phone ring, and again he heard his name called. This time it was the owner of a neighborhood diner who had heard of his plight from his customers, and wanted to know if he could help. Everyone in his neighborhood knew Billy. Billy was so moved by the man's compassion and concern that he began thanking him over and over for calling. The "I'll be okay, I'll be okay" refrain began going through his mind again.

Once more the phone rang, and this time it was Billy's friend, Connie. He called to tell Billy that he would be on the evening news. They would be doing a "bridge story." At last, Billy thought. I will be a hero when they watch me on the news. Life will be different. The residents, the nurses, the orderlies, even the doctors, they will all respect me. They'll see I'm not crazy, that I don't belong here. Then they'll let me out.

As he was talking with Connie, Billy noticed a resident in a straight jacket who had been sleeping on a stretcher. When he got off the phone, Billy went to him and heard him, whispering, "Water, water." Billy listened to him for awhile, then went to the nurses station. "This man wants some water," Billy told a nurse.

"He can't have any," the nurse said. "He gets wild."

Billy went back and began talking to the man. This was the first time Billy had ever seen anyone in a straight jacket, and he was both fascinated by it and sorry for the poor guy. He continued talking to the man and made him promise that he would be good if the nurses let him out and gave him water.

Billy went back to the nurses and told them, "Please let him out. He promised he would be good." For some reason the nurses believed Billy and took off the jacket. The man slowly began moving around and got his drink of water. Billy watched him as he began to break his promise and got violent. As the man picked up a chair, Billy continued to watch in a detached way. His mind was on the 5 o'clock news. He couldn't wait. He would see to it that everyone watched the news. When the man threw the chair at the TV, Billy thought, Oh well, there goes the TV!

Billy continued to watch the clock. It was 4:40 p.m. The news was coming on soon. The news? But wait! The TV! Oh, no! There would be no 5 o'clock news for Billy, or for anyone on sixth floor of Bellevue Mental Hospital. No one here would learn about the man who had snarled traffic for five and one-half hours in an attempt to be heard. No one here would know the mistake that had been made in bringing this man here. No one would hear. Billy groaned, "Why the TV? Why me?" At that moment, Billy became just another inmate, another Thorazine puppet. He picked up the little chant in his mind again: "Tick, tock, tick, tock, three more days I'll see the doc."

And with no news . . . now for the sports. Billy watched as nurses wrestled with the destroyer of his destiny, the man who smashed the TV, returning him to his straight jacket.

CHAPTER 3

Roots – The Sins of the Fathers

Billy's dramatic plea for help was, ultimately, in vain. Billy gained momentary fame, the eyes of all New York City on him for one desperate day, but he was looking for help in the wrong direction. Neither religion nor psychiatry could offer him the solution to his problems. Not only could they not solve his problems, the practitioners and professionals did not seem to care. People made promises they had no intention of keeping. "We'll get you help" were merely words spoken in an attempt to get him out of the way, off the bridge, so their lives could go on.

After all the hype of that one day – the snarled traffic, the news on TV throughout the day, the newspaper headlines – Billy Schneider, his 15 minutes of fame spent, went back to being just Billy Schneider, dope fiend. Nobody had listened, and nobody cared. His circumstances were, if anything, worse than ever. Being labeled "insane" and spending three days as a Thorazine robot, then being discharged with only a warning to avoid high places, had no positive effect. It only made change seem even more impossible.

Billy's mom, Helen, unable to visit him in the hospital, went with Terri to pick him up when he was discharged. Recovering from back surgery, she had been resting in bed three days earlier when she heard this report on the radio – "One young fellow doesn't want to see the rest of this beautiful spring day . . ." She did not catch a name, but her motherly intuition told her it was Billy who had scaled the George Washington Bridge. When she found he had been taken to Bellevue, she tried to visit, but was told he was "intolerable." Now, thrilled that her son had survived his ordeal, Helen gave in to his insistence that he drive them home. His brain still on a Thorazine pillow, he made this one scary ride for the women.

And his father? In a gin mill, he sat watching the news on TV when someone cried, "Sonny! That's your kid on the bridge!" From his TV-side bar stool, Sonny Schneider's response was, "Jump! Go ahead and jump!"

To understand Billy Schneider, one must first know his roots. Where he came from has a great deal to do with where he has gone. Climbing the George Washington Bridge was not merely the result of a one-night stand with cocaine. It was more than frustration with the Methadone program. It went far beyond the fact that his current friend Terri was too tired to listen to him.

No, his present circumstances had much more to do with a childhood of abuse and neglect, of living with alcoholism and rage. For Billy, the streets of New York City often were safer than the sanctuary of his home. It had to do with the negative influences of early life heroes, such as his Uncle Sonny. Billy's early adulthood already had been filled with drug use, crime, illicit sex, unstable relationships and prison.

Furthermore, his parents had also grown up with abuse, with neglect, with alcoholism. Truly, the sins committed against his parents were passed on to the children.

Consider Billy's mom. Beaten and abused as a child, a "little mother" to her nine younger siblings, she grew up amid hostility. Her own mother thought nothing of throwing things at her children. Her father beat the children, showing no apparent remorse. Helen remembers her father as easier to live with when he was drunk. Her memories of childhood are not pleasant.

Running away from her home, she was married and pregnant by the age of sixteen. Helen bears emotional scars from this relationship, which perhaps was even more abusive than her childhood home had been. After her first son Bobby was born, she fled once again, to protect both herself and her son. Still a teenager, she fell into yet another abusive relationship, this time with the man who became Billy's and Danny's father, William "Sonny" Schneider.

Billy's dad also grew up in a home filled with violence and alcoholism. He was a small man, about five foot six. Was he just repeating what was done to him, or was he trying to compensate for his small stature? Whatever the reason, Sonny became a person to be feared, not only in his home by Helen and his three sons, but by all who knew him. He seemed to live for physical fights, picking them with anyone who crossed him.

Violence was the norm for Sonny, both at home and on the streets. He often came home in the early hours of the morning, drunk, and would wake his young sons in order to show off to his buddies. Billy has memories of being placed on top of the refrigerator in the middle of the night and being ordered to jump. In terror, both of his father and of the jump, he would do so, only to be hurt as he fell to the floor, as his father rarely caught him. Returning to bed with bloodied lip or nose, he would cry himself back to sleep, wondering, "Why does he do that?"

Divorce was not an easy option in the 1940s, and Helen was not able to obtain one. So, while intentions were good, Sonny and Helen lived in a common-law relationship, never able to legally marry. Billy was born, then, into an environment that was both sinful and violent. In the 1940s, an unwed situation was far more rare than it is in the 1990s and carried with it a tremendous sense of shame. Helen felt keen shame about the relationship, often using the Schneider name. Her feelings were heightened all the more because of the abuse she again received from the person who should have been her provider and protector.

Helen was beaten often at the hands of Sonny. And Sonny worked only periodically. When he was employed, he usually drove an ice truck, but was fired frequently because of his violent temper. He spent most of what he earned on alcohol, so the responsibility for the care of the family inevitably fell on Helen. Sporadically the family had use of a car, which would be abandoned when it broke down or was wrecked.

Helen did her best to provide for her three sons. In order to pay the rent, she became superintendent of the apartment complex in which they lived. It was hard work, and the young Schneider boys helped her by picking up trash and sorting through paper, separating newspapers from magazines for paper sales. In this way, Billy was introduced to pornography by the age of eight. Other men's trash became Billy's mental garbage.

Helen loved her sons. But the sins of the parents visited themselves on her, and she repeated much of what she had grown up with. Partying was a pastime for her and Sonny. Perhaps alcohol temporarily would soothe some of the internal pain and rage she felt, caused by past as well as present abuses. It was a hard life for Helen, from having an eye blackened by her father when she was two months old to seeing her sons sent off to prison.

It was not unusual for the Schneider boys to be beaten or for them to witness their mother beaten. At bedtime, Sonny often would stand at the doorway, threatening them, no matter whether or not he had a reason.

The boys would have to walk by him to enter their bedroom. As they dashed past him, they never knew where or how they would be hit: the mouth, the stomach, the eyes, sometimes with a fist, other times a belt. He was a small man in his adult world, but Sonny was large in the eyes of his young sons. One can only imagine the thoughts that went through their young minds as night after night they would go through their father's torture machine to bed.

At other times Sonny might express his rage by overturning the dinner table if he was dissatisfied with the meal or with the boys' behavior at meal times. Of course, it always was Helen who cleaned up the mess afterward.

As a child, Billy was sensitive and timid, but crying was a mark of weakness to Dad. He used Billy's tears as an excuse to be rough and cruel. "I'm just trying to beat the fear out of Billy," he would say. More damaging to Billy than the physical wounding was the wounding of his spirit. Early on he started being hard and tough himself, a cover-up for the hurt he felt inside. This may have been true for his father, as well. Sonny's brutality may have covered the pain he carried from his own past abuse. No one ever could get beneath Sonny's shell-like exterior to find out, and sad to say, Sonny Schneider likely died with no one understanding his pain.

Billy was raised a Catholic, going to mass regularly. He even served as an altar boy while in prison at Rikers Island. But as he looks back on those years, he realizes he never once heard the good news that Jesus bled and died for his salvation.

Billy has few memories of his childhood. Some of those memories are unhappy, but there were good times, too. Billy remembers his dad buying a pool table for the boys for Christmas and teaching them all to play. Billy still loves to play pool. In fact, he often earned his daily sustenance playing pool. (One of Billy's jingles went: "Pool's my game on the street, I did it for my bread and meat. If I didn't win, I didn't eat.")

Sometimes Sonny and Helen took the boys fishing or to the beach. But even these good times were strictly regimented and laced with fear of dad's anger.

Then there was Christmas Eve of 1959 when Sonny and Helen went shopping for gifts, stopping off in a bar on the way home. While seated on the bar stools, Sonny caught a man stealing the packages at their feet. He whipped up his fist to stop him, not realizing that the man was armed. Sonny was stabbed, and when the boys woke up the next morning it was their dad who was wrapped up instead of presents. This incident had a very disturbing impact on Sonny, and from that time on abuse in the Schneider home worsened significantly. Sonny was not used to losing a fight. A seething bitterness toward his assailant may have been the reason for such an increase in his cruelty.

When Billy was seventeen, his dad moved out of their home. He lived with other women and continued his unstable and unhealthy lifestyle. By this time Billy was already in trouble with the law. On one occasion, when Billy faced juvenile detention, he was released by the judge when Helen told him that Billy's father was no longer in the home. After this, Billy had little to do with his dad.

That meant the most significant adult male in Billy's life was his Uncle Sonny. His mom's younger brother, only about six years older than Billy, Alfred "Sonny" Kern often lived with his sister Helen. Wild and flashy, he was far more interesting to Billy than was his own father. He was so charming that his sister refused to believe he could do any wrong. As the boys grew up, Sonny often hung out with them and their friends. He had beautiful eyes, making the neighborhood girls fantasize about him. He drove a nice car, which made the Schneider boys feel important. They all looked up to Uncle Sonny. Truly he was one of Billy's heroes, but, sad to say, not a positive one.

It was Uncle Sonny who began to lead his nephews into a life of crime. He bragged about time in prison and taught the boys prison card games. It was Uncle Sonny who taught Billy the techniques of breaking and entering. He was a common criminal, a petty thief. Considering himself a modern-day Robin Hood, he bragged that he would steal from the rich and give to the poor. It was a self-interested philosophy, though, as he apparently regarded himself as one of the poor, and felt it his right to take what he pleased. He seemed to have no conscience. On several occasions, he let one of his nephews take the rap for his crimes, never taking responsibility or voicing any remorse over it.

Another person who exerted a very negative influence on Billy early in life was a man named Frank. A buddy of Billy's father, Frank spent a lot of time in the Schneider home. Dad and Mother thought nothing of putting a drunken Frank across the end of the boys' bed for the night. One night ten-year-old Billy awoke to this man fondling him beneath the covers. He was confused by what was happening – horrified both with what Frank was doing and the feeling it aroused in him. By a single act of sexual abuse, Billy was pulled away from coloring books and toward pornography. What he had already seen in pictures came to life for him, destroying forever the innocence of childhood. Billy soon learned that allowing this man to touch him gained him favors. Money, candy, and food came his way. Billy's desire for those things competed with his sense of shame over what was happening. Deepening his feelings of shame was the fact that it felt good to him. He found himself being drawn to touch this man, which made him feel as though he were the sinner. Finally, mother witnessed Frank sexually "playing" with Billy, which put a stop to the behavior. Frank disappeared from the Schneider home, and Helen sought help from John, a lawyer who was dating one of Sonny's sisters. John treated the situation with sensitivity, speaking kindly to Billy and talking things over with Billy and his mom. But his family began calling Billy names – "faggot," "homo," or "queer." The labels stuck and stung Billy. And it made Billy begin to wonder just who and what he was.

The sexual abuse had a tremendous impact on Billy, sharply increasing his feelings of insecurity and shame. Later in life it would come back to haunt him, pulling him in directions that he may not otherwise have chosen. The labels echoed in his mind: "You faggot! You homo!" It would be years before the issue could be put to rest.

CHAPTER 4

Jumping into a Life of Crime

T he three Schneider boys spent much of their time on the streets, playing games, getting into fights, and eventually becoming involved in neighborhood gangs. Billy aspired to be as tough as his father. He wasn't about to let bigger bullies get the best of him. He was small, but quick and agile. His punches were hard and found their mark. Others began to respect him.

When he was about twelve, Billy had his first encounter with the police. In some ways the police took the place of his parents in being disciplinarians. Beatings are a poor substitute for an upbringing, and Billy needed to be brought up. A father showing compassion and love was lacking in Billy's life. The result was disorder.

In Billy's first brush with the police, the authorities played a nurturing role. In the future, their involvement would be restrictive, and, sometimes, abusive. Billy and Danny planned a fishing trip. Leaving early in the morning with their fishing poles and puppy, they headed across the George Washington Bridge into New Jersey. Climbing down the Palisades Englewood Cliffs, directly across the river from home, they had taken neither money nor lunch. They had not had breakfast either. It was a rather long trek, but they made their way to the river and happily began fishing.

Boys and puppy were having a great time, but soon they became hungry. Looking around, Billy spotted an apple tree. This could provide brunch, so Billy began to climb the tree to pick apples. With his shirt full, the branch under him suddenly gave way, and Billy came crashing to the ground. As he stood up, he was thoroughly alarmed to see a limb protruding from his chest. In panic, the boys ran to a man fishing nearby. The fisherman took one look at Billy, covered Billy's eyes, and, giving the branch a jerk, pulled it out of his chest. He then summoned the Palisades State Park Police, who in turn notified the Englewood City Police.

Soon, off in the distance, Billy heard a siren wail, the first of many that would be turned on for him. Billy, Danny, and puppy were placed in the back seat of the police car and taken to the Englewood Hospital Emergency Room. While the nurses cleaned and dressed Billy's wound, which fortunately was not deep enough to injure his lungs, the police obtained all necessary information and called the boys' parents. The nurses were smitten by these two cute boys and their puppy, and when they learned that this had happened because they were hungry, they scurried to the kitchen, bringing the boys a lunch and a big bone for the puppy.

When Mom and Dad came to pick them up, Sonny showed no sympathy and called Billy stupid. He apparently felt little shame that his sons had left home hungry because there was no food in the house.

By the time he was twelve, Billy had picked up his first addiction: cigarettes. Along with the cigarettes, he picked up a nasty attitude. He thought he was cool and tough. Actually, he was just a tender boy trying to be tough in a cruel world. Always the class clown, he easily led others into mischief. With a quick wit and a way with words, he began earning the nickname given him later in life – "Billy Words." At the same time, he began to experiment with sniffing airplane glue and other inhalants. Billy's use of stimulants progressed rapidly from sniffing glue to drinking alcohol and smoking marijuana.

Billy performed poorly in school. When the family moved from the Bronx to Manhattan, Billy was not enrolled into a new school for some time, causing him to fail the third grade. From then on, he continued to fall behind. In the future, some of his favorite pastimes would become games such as Monopoly, Chess and Scrabble. But the names "stupid" and "dumb," as his father called him, moved from ears to brain to heart. The man who should have been building up Billy did nothing but tear him down. The power of the father/son relationship was not lost on young Billy. Otherwise, the name-calling, the put-downs, the fear instilled, might have been less influential. Even now, Billy will wonder aloud, "I have a good brain, don't I?" It's his way of seeking reassurance.

When Billy was fourteen or fifteen, he ran away from home for the first time, along with Danny and friend Richie. The three young boys met two homosexual men on their neighborhood streets and promised to go to bed with them for money. These men took the boys to their home, engaging them in sexual behaviors, but they were both so drunk they fell asleep before they could pay and dismiss the boys. The boys went through their pockets and ripped them off, leaving with several hundred dollars. Feeling no guilt, they jumped on a train and went to Atlantic City. But their lark ended in disaster. Looking suspicious because they were flashing so much money, the boys were picked up by the police and placed in jail overnight while their parents were called. The police could not confiscate the money, since they did not know where it came from. Sonny, hearing there was money involved, came to get them and confiscated it himself, then all the way home threatened his sons with a beating. Dad never asked where the money came from, or whether there was anything the boys needed to make right. He drove the boys home, unaware of the criminal sexual behaviors that had been perpetrated against his sons.

At sixteen, Billy had finished seventh grade. The streets were more exciting to him than the classroom, and he often played hooky. At his age, being in the eighth grade was discouraging. Billy could see no value in continuing his education and dropped out. This gave him something he didn't need – time, and the opportunity to spend it without guidance. He was not ready for this, even though he thought so. The streets became his classroom; his peers and Uncle Sonny became his teachers.

About this time, Billy noticed a young girl named Linda Foell who, along with her older brother, Jimmy, hung out at Washington Heights Park and a local coffee house, Bickford's. Linda already was experimenting with drugs at the age of 12 or 13. Even so, Billy's heart beat a bit faster at the sight of her lovely blonde hair and sweet ways.

Billy decided to ask Linda for a date. Unbeknownst to him, a mutual "friend" had warned Linda to beware of Billy. He told her that Billy would take her into the park and rape her. Unaware of this, Billy innocently asked if she would like to take a walk with him – in the park, no less! Linda must have had a streak of daring in her, as she accepted this invitation, her heart pounding. She was amazed at Billy's gentleness, and relieved when the only advance he made was to shyly hold her hand. Enchanted by his charisma and humor, she continued to see him after he walked her home safely from their first date.

Billy also was arrested for the first time at sixteen. In the wrong neighborhood, Billy found himself surrounded by an Irish rival gang called the "Tiny Tots." Realizing his dangerous predicament, he searched desperately for a way out. At first he did not see a solution. But suddenly, like an angel, Richard Availes, a 16-year-old Hispanic friend, appeared in a 1964 Plymouth station wagon. Richard was a former member of Billy's gang, the "Terrace Boys." Billy made a dash for the car, jumped in, and Richard sped away. As the fear of danger subsided, Billy learned that Richard had stolen the car from a Safeway Supermarket while the driver was delivering groceries. A new disaster! But wait – why not have a little fun? The boys took the car on a joy ride, picking up friends throughout the neighborhood and driving around until 10 p.m., when they parked the car outside the store, leaving the keys inside. What could be so wrong with that, the boys thought.

Later the same night, Billy was picked up by the 34th precinct police and brought in for questioning. Out of innocence or naiveté, he pleaded guilty to the same crime as Richard did. His greatest fear was not of being booked and finger-printed; it was facing his father should he find out. The police told him that if he would plead guilty and sign a "youthful offender" agreement, (now called "conditional discharge") he would be placed on three years' probation for possession of a stolen car. He would be released in the morning, when he would go before the judge. This sounded good to Billy. He thought he could "get away with it" and his father would never find out.

This agreement was soon to backfire on Billy. If probation were broken at any time, Billy automatically would receive three years in prison.

Less than two years later, Billy was arrested. On his eighteenth birthday, with his mother in the courtroom, Billy was sentenced to three years in Rikers Island for possession of $5 worth of marijuana. Looking more like a boy of twelve, Billy stood before the judge, handcuffed and shackled. As he shuffled past his mom on the way out, he looked at the clock on the wall. It was 2 p.m. He wondered what she was thinking. Was she remembering that very moment eighteen years earlier when the doctor had placed her squalling newborn son in her arms? How could any mom, cradling her brand new baby, anticipate that child going to prison later in life? His mom says it was the worst day of her life, the day when one of her sons first went to prison.

Unfortunately, prison was to become a way of life for Billy. On this noteworthy day, the day that emancipates a minor, one's eighteenth birthday, Billy entered a very hostile adult world. If he thought he was tough on the streets, he now had to be tough in a whole new way in order to survive.

Although Billy considered himself a "peacenik," he was not into anti-Vietnam demonstrations, nor was he anti-American in his thinking. He would have preferred to go to Vietnam than prison. But the judge would have none of this. Billy was instead classified 4-F (unfit for military service) and labeled a drug addict. With yet another negative label, Billy was ushered into a different war.

CHAPTER 5

Prison 101:
An Introduction to
Life in Rikers Island

Billy entered the adult world of the New York City Men's
Reformatory, known as Rikers Island. There, he began to pay, in
a big way, for signing the "youthful offender" agreement out of
fear of his father. His father was no longer a part of his life, but his long
fingers of negative influence continued to shape Billy and his destiny.

Prison is a place of unimaginable evil, as Billy soon learned. When
incarcerated criminals behave badly, there is genuine reason for fear. It
is not easy to be a prisoner. Prison is not a refuge or a place to be taken
lightly. Billy, with his wit and words as well as his tough body, gained the
respect of many of his fellow prisoners. His African-American "brothers" found this "cracker" (prison slang for a white boy) hilarious. Men
twice Billy's size were outsmarted verbally, Billy making them understand the folly of beating him to a pulp, which could so easily happen
behind bars. "If you do beat a little guy like me, what will you have to
brag about? But if I beat you instead, you will never live it down." Billy
made it clear from the moment he entered prison, and each time he
reentered, that he was "SSBP," – "Skinny, Small, But Powerful."

"I'm Billy Words, down by law; you mess with me, I'll break your jaw,"
became his motto. There were men here who knew his uncles, Johnny
(his father's brother) and Sonny, both of them having spent time at
Rikers before Billy. This helped to give him a break.

America was in the midst of racial unrest, and what happened on the
streets was intensified in the prisons. The 1960s was the era of Malcolm
X, of Black Muslims, of Martin Luther King, Jr. and the segregation
issue. Billy learned that racial prejudice in prison could be violent, even

deadly. This kind of atmosphere and thinking was foreign to Billy. He always had African-American and Hispanic friends. But in prison, if a white man crossed over to the African-American community, even a black man might hate him. In the perverted logic of prison, the message was, "If his own people don't want him, then neither do we." Despite his wit and natural affinity for people, Billy learned to be careful.

When Billy arrived at Rikers, he had a private cell. Soon, however, the prison became more crowded, and inmates were doubled up. His first cell mate turned out to be an Albino man of African-American heritage, a formula for difficulty in this racially turbulent arena. The man was hostile toward Billy, calling him the devil. Billy in turn called him "Casper," which infuriated him. Soon their anger flamed into an all-out brawl, and Billy's roommate was moved to a different cell.

What did Billy learn in prison? The good thing was that he earned his GED. The rest was not so good. Exposed to violence, pornography, and crime, he became more of a criminal behind bars. He was daring and naturally intuitive, which led him to do things such as the following "B&E," accomplished right under the noses of the prison guards.

Rikers Island has identical upper and lower tiers, with guards' stations in the center of two long quadrants placed at right angles to one another. In this center area was a laundry room, and one of Billy's prison mates found that a grill in the wall could be removed. This grill covered a duct that led directly to the laundry room below. "Billy," this friend said, "you are small enough that you could fit through this duct. You know the lower tier is empty from 8 a.m. to 3 p.m." Billy got the picture. When the time was right, and with the help of his friend, he slipped through the duct and into the laundry room below. From there it was simple to get right into the unattended guards' station and hit a lever, releasing all the cell doors. Billy randomly opened cells and took whatever he could find – cigarettes, magazines, food items. Then he flipped the lever locking the cells and went back the way he came. No one was the wiser, but the upper tier heard from the "land down under!" While upper inmates enjoyed the spoils, suspicion grew and fights broke out below. Those from whom nothing had been taken became the objects of this suspicion.

Billy, although he was small, was muscular, and the guard in charge of the gym, Mr. Isaacs, noticed his natural muscle definition. One day he called Billy into the weight room and made an example of his body to the weight-lifting team, letting them know that Billy had naturally what they did not, despite all their hours of workouts. "Look at this body! This is what you are all working for." He began to work with Billy to increase his muscle mass, which Billy never had worked on. He was given special favors, including being allowed double portions at meal times. This attention did him no good. It merely turned him into a wiseguy, a punk with an attitude.

Billy learned how to do tattoos, and, being artistic, he tattooed his own body. Others soon had him working on their bodies, as well. Burned toilet paper, mixed with water, provided ink. A safety pin, a sewing needle, or a staple removed from a magazine center and sharpened on the cement floor provided a needle for the job. A pen with ink and ball point removed made a handle – the plastic was easily melted using a match or lighter and the needle inserted into the hot plastic.

Doing tattoos in prison was not legal and Billy spent seven days in solitary – "The Bing" – when he had to be treated for an infected tattoo.

Inmates do not put their sexuality to sleep. In a group of criminals, some of whom are incarcerated for sex-related crimes, sexuality can create a highly volatile situation. While some men in prison could be called homosexual, many inmates perform homosexual acts just because of a lack of female companionship. A male who in any way appears timid or weak becomes a target for prison rape. However, by no means is all sexual activity done violently. Billy was vulnerable in this area, having been exposed to sexual advances from a male as a child. The charm and mystery seen in his twinkling brown eyes attracted both men and women to him. A man he often played cards with said to him one day, "You have such awesome eyes." It was said in a flirtatious way, perhaps as a test, but when Billy did not respond it went no further.

While in line for meals, another inmate began blowing kisses at Billy. They passed each other daily, meal after meal, and each time Billy would be blown a kiss. This infuriated Billy, and he sought for a way to show this man that he would not tolerate his behavior. If he did not set boundaries with this inmate, he would be a target for other men. One day, Billy had gotten his tray when he saw this inmate still seated. Sure enough, he blew Billy a kiss. Without giving away his intentions with body language, Billy made his way to the inmate's table. When he was right behind him, Billy slammed his dinner tray down onto his head. The man slumped as food went flying. A mini-riot had to be broken up by the guards, and Billy spent thirty days in solitary. But from that day on, he was left alone, not only by this inmate, but by any others who might have had similar thoughts. His reputation was established by this incident. There was no mistaking Billy's message.

In prison, other inmates were not the only source of danger. A guard dragged Billy from his bed one morning because he missed the count. Ignoring the fact that Billy was sick, he was determined to punish him: several lashes across the buttocks with a broom handle. When Billy fainted before the beating, dripping with perspiration from a fever, another guard intervened and brought him to the infirmary.

While in Rikers Island, Billy found the poem "King Heroin" inscribed on his cell wall by a previous inmate. He committed it to memory, and many who know Billy have heard him quote it. Although he had not yet had a taste of this mighty king of drugs, the poem should have been a warning to him.

Life with its tragedies continued on the outside while men did time on the inside. Billy was in prison with a man whose wife and daughter were found strangled while he was behind bars. One can barely imagine the helpless rage that would come with finding oneself in the position this father and husband did.

Billy was paroled from Rikers Island after fourteen months, on August 13, 1968, with the "youthful offender" agreement still in effect. If he broke parole, he would be returned to prison to complete the three-year sentence.

CHAPTER 6

Uncle Sonny's Influence

Billy's mom, happy to have her son home, threw a belated 19th birthday party for him. That night, Billy was introduced to LSD. A drink laced by a friend turned him wild. He became disorderly, rude, and loud, breaking one of his mom's favorite records during the party. His mother was dismayed by this new Billy, thinking his behavior must be a result of time spent in prison. Billy had by this time been introduced to heavier drugs. He was willing to take anything that could be swallowed, snorted or sniffed. Many pills were available on the streets. But LSD was different. A concoction that caused an "acid trip," this drug was new and dangerous, frightening even to Billy.

Toughened by his time in prison, Billy again took to the streets, under the influence of his Uncle Sonny, who seemed perversely pleased that his young nephews were following in his footsteps. Charismatic as he was, he charmed them into a sinful belief system: crime was okay as long as you didn't get caught and as long as you did not injure anyone. If you meant no harm you were not truly a criminal. If you took from the rich to help the poor (yourself), that was an act to improve a distorted society. Besides, what was wrong with having a little fun? Uncle Sonny stole to help out his family, and he was so charming about it that his family could see no wrong in what he did. He even convinced his nephews that it was heroic when they took the rap for him, which they did on more than one occasion. Not even the boys' mother could speak up on their behalf when she knew this to be true.

Billy's older brother Bobby's first arrest was for one of Uncle Sonny's crimes. Sonny walked into a shoemaker's shop one morning, and when the owner went to the back of the store, Sonny made off with the cash register. The shoemaker saw red. Red shirts, that is. It happened that both Sonny and Bobby wore red shirts that day. The shoemaker identified the wrong red shirt, and it was Bobby who was picked up by the 34th precinct police. Identified, fingerprinted and booked as the criminal, 16-year-old Bobby sat, while Uncle Sonny remained the rat, never speaking up.

Sonny always seemed to slip away while the nephews were left holding the bag. One night, when Billy was 19 and just three months after he had been released from Rikers Island, Sonny left the bar where his sister Helen was working, itching for a little excitement. He woke up Billy at home saying, "Come on, let's pull a B&E!" He led Billy to what they thought was the back door of a gin mill. In reality, they were entering the back door to a pharmacy housed in the same building as the gin mill. They must have set off an alarm, and at 5 a.m. a shot rang out on Broadway. Billy and Sonny ran, and as Billy heard the echo of the shot meant for him, he had an eerie feeling. A new sense of fear was added to the life of crime he was falling into. He heard someone shouting for him to stop. Ironically, he had just been telling Sonny he had never been shot at. Just as ironically, Sonny got away, while Billy tried to convince the police that he had been trying to break into a gin mill for money from cigarette machines and pool tables and not for drugs from the pharmacy. Discovering that Billy already had been incarcerated because of drugs, the authorities were convinced he was trying to get into the pharmacy.

It really made no difference what he had been up to. He had broken conditions of parole, so on November 21, 1968, his mother's birthday, he was returned to Rikers Island to serve the remainder of the three-year sentence under the "youthful offender" agreement he had signed at age sixteen. It was a heavy price to pay for avoiding his father's wrath. Billy called his mother, saying, "Happy Birthday, Mom. I'm going back to prison."

Shortly after he arrived at Rikers Island for the second time, a prison riot broke out, reinforcing what Billy already knew. Prison was not safe. A man incarcerated at Rikers had a sister who had been raped. The rapist was caught, and due to overcrowding in the city jail, Rikers Island was being used as a holding area. Although he would never have been sentenced to the same prison, the rapist was sent to Rikers Island while awaiting trial. The brother vowed to kill the rapist if he ever came in contact with him. Consequently, they were housed in different areas. But a slip was made on movie day – they both attended at the same time. Violence broke out when the brother saw the rapist. Folding chairs went flying. Everyone was in immediate danger. Billy, with his keen senses, quickly exited the room, just a step ahead of the guards. The room was locked, and the remaining inmates were sprayed with tear gas, quelling what could have become an all-out riot.

After 13 months, Billy once again was released, in December, 1969. He had served a total of 27 months under the "youthful offender" act for a crime (possession of marijuana) that carried with it a maximum one-year sentence. He was released nine months early due to a writ of habeas corpus, which also freed 800 other prisoners. In response to a fellow prisoner's suit, the Supreme Court ruled that it was a violation of people's rights to serve three years under the Youthful Offender Act for a crime which carried a maximum penalty of fewer than three years. Billy was at last freed as well from the penalty of having feared his father. Even so, the idea that he had been incarcerated for 27 months because of his father was a dangerous way of thinking. Billy had become a criminal in his own right, and while he otherwise may not have served so long for the crimes committed, he nevertheless had broken the law.

And while Billy was in prison, life outside had gone on. Billy continued to have a relationship with Linda Foell. Her father had died unexpectedly in 1968, when Linda was 15. This was devastating both for her and her brother, Jimmy. Linda withdrew from her mom, and began to use drugs more heavily. Her mom, having no idea about the drugs, took her to California the following summer to visit Disneyland and other attractions. Having family fun, her mom thought, was a way for both of them to get relief from the difficulties of the past year, and she hoped the time together would strengthen their relationship. But she was unable to get close to her daughter. She thought Linda had a cold, when in reality the sniffles were caused by drug withdrawal. Linda never confided in her mom. She couldn't wait to get home and back to the drugs that seemed to give her relief.

Life for Billy's mom was changing as well. While Billy was at Rikers Island, Helen moved to the Bronx, followed by Bobby, Danny and Uncle Sonny. She began to date a man named Porzio. Porzio was a long-time friend of the family, first as a "heroin buddy" to Sonny Schneider's brother, Johnny. He also had married (and later divorced) one of Sonny's sisters. He treated Helen like a queen, caring for her in a way she had never before been cared for. He was charming, had a nice home in New Jersey, had a trade and money. It was not long before Helen was deeply in love.

Billy moved into his mom's Bronx apartment after his release. A short time later, Helen moved to New Jersey with Porzio, leaving the three boys and their Uncle Sonny in her apartment.

Just days after his second release from Rikers Island, Billy and Uncle Sonny were on the prowl, breaking into a neighborhood grocery store. Billy got caught, while Sonny got away with the groceries. Helen suspected Sonny, but, once again, did not confront him.

Meanwhile, Sonny, knowing where Billy was headed with the police, took the express train to Canal Street to a place familiar by now both to him and his family – the Manhattan Criminal Court. Criminal activity in Manhattan is so common the courts are open seven days a week, twenty-four hours a day. Sonny, also familiar with procedures, realized both when and where the case of the City of New York vs. William C. Schneider would be held. So he sat in the courtroom amid the free, and definitely the brave, trusting his nephew not to rat on him.

Ten men were led into the courtroom, Billy among them. When he spotted his uncle/hero, he informed his legal aide, his court appointed lawyer, that his uncle was present and in court. This was always a plus for anyone going before a judge in the New York City system. So when the judge asked, "Does the defendant have anyone in his family present in the court room?" Billy's lawyer cried in reply, "Yes, your honor, The defendant's uncle, Alfred Kern, is present for the defendant. Would your honor consider releasing the defendant on his own recognizance, to the custody of his uncle?"

The judge was snowed, and off went the two criminals. Billy and his hero were back in the saddle again.

Hours later, same night, same borough, same court, same Billy, same Uncle Sonny stood before same judge for attempted burglary. His honor, the judge, was stunned when the charges were read by the bailiff. "Didn't I just release this guy? I must be getting tired! Let's all rise for recess!" Sonny was the one who usually got away, but not this time. And Billy? He spent sixteen days in the Brooklyn House of Detention because there was no one to pay bail. Then he was released to the custody of his mother, the case against him dropped because the witness, a Russian-speaking building superintendent, made an error with his English. When asked where and how he first saw Billy, he replied with his heavy Russian accent, "I first saw him standing in the sleeping position."How's that again? The judge must have decided that he should believe nothing further, and he dropped the charges.

The four young men continued living in Helen's Bronx apartment, Sonny returning there after a short stay in jail. But Sonny was not content to do well, and one evening he decided to have a little fun. Between Helen's apartment and the apartment next door was a dumbwaiter shared by both apartments, a kind of an elevator to the basement used for trash disposal. Sonny opened his side of the dumbwaiter and kicked in the doors on the neighbor's side, planning a burglary. He had been drinking and meant no harm. But what did he think the outcome would be, no matter how one looked at it? Who would get into an apartment through the dumbwaiter except someone from the apartment sharing it?

Without realizing that someone was home on the other side, Sonny came crashing through. He very quickly made his way back through the dumbwaiter and exited his own apartment. Meanwhile Bobby, the innocent nephew sleeping in his own living room, woke up when he heard something going on. When the neighbors began to investigate the noises heard from their side of the dumbwaiter, who should be peering back at them but Bobby? Once again, Uncle Sonny got away and Bobby took the rap, spending two months in detention. This incident brought an end to the party in Helen's apartment, and Billy went to live with his mom and Porzio.

After this, Billy did not have as much to do with his uncle. And what became of Uncle Sonny? In the mid-1980s, he killed a man, according to evidence and what he said to those who knew him best. His brother Eddie found the gun said to be used as the murder weapon. Sonny was working as superintendent of an apartment building in the Bronx. He and a friend were drinking when they heard something. Going to investigate, they caught a 21-year-old Hispanic man breaking into the building. He was a common thief, just like Uncle Sonny. Only Sonny didn't see it that way and took the law into his own hands. The young man had a knife and apparently did not drop it when Sonny ordered him to. Sonny shot him. Leaving him where he was, the friends went back to drinking. Later they returned and realized he was still alive, so in order to put him out of his misery, Sonny shot him again, fatally this time. Then they tried to dispose of the body by throwing it in the furnace. Sonny was arrested, however, and sent to Rikers Island to await trial. After about a year and a half, he came to trial but was released, found not guilty on a technicality. And Sonny bragged, "I beat the big one!"

But did he? On February 6, 1986, Sonny, in his early 40s, became ill and went to the hospital. Only 18 hours later, on a stretcher and alone in the emergency room hallway of Northside General Hospital in New York City, Sonny died. At first it was attributed to cardiac arrest, but an autopsy showed that Sonny died of AIDS-related pneumonia. Had Sonny known? If so, he carried the secret almost to the grave with him.

The director of the funeral home, poorly informed about the virus that causes AIDS, cautioned family and friends not to touch the body lest they be infected. Along with a fear of the disease, there was great ignorance about the means of its transmission a decade ago.

On hearing of his death, Sonny's sisters got together to tell their mother, accompanied by Billy. At first, Mom was thrilled to see her four daughters visiting her. But almost immediately she sensed that something must be wrong, for these sisters had not spoken to one another for years. She cried, "He's dead, isn't he? My Eddie's dead!" Her youngest son, Eddie, had been missing for six months, presumed either dead or having disappeared with a Hare Krishna group. Slightly retarded, he also was depressed and had spoken often of suicide. But no. This day, it was Sonny.

Just a year later, the family discovered that Eddie was buried in the "potter's field," a graveyard for unidentified persons. He had been found earlier in the Hudson River, just below the George Washington Bridge. His body had been brought to the police morgue and his clothing and identification placed in a bag, awaiting notification of the family. Meanwhile, the precinct police department was in the process of moving. Somehow Eddie's clothes and identification were separated from his body, and he was left as unidentified. Thus, he was buried in the potter's field. Much later, his clothing and identification were found, and the family was notified. His body was exhumed and buried next to Sonny's. The family assumed that Eddie committed suicide.

CHAPTER 7

Satan's Web

Billy not only was powerfully influenced by his Uncle Sonny; his life also was bent by Porzio, a man who at first seemed to hold out a silver spoon. But soon it was clear there was an evil, even Satanic twist to this man.

By Christmas of 1969, Helen was living in Porzio's home. After Sonny's "dumb" dumbwaiter incident, forcing the young men to move out of Helen's apartment, she invited Billy to New Jersey to be with her and Porzio. Porzio offered Billy a job, and it looked like a way out for Billy, so he accepted. Helen was excited about him coming. She wanted to make up for lost time and she lavished holiday gifts on him.

Porzio was a master plumber, and Billy quickly learned the trade from him. But he soon learned Porzio was a master deceiver as well. When Billy found Porzio eyeing him strangely, he recognized the look. He had seen it in prison. He began testing Porzio, and soon Porzio was "out of the closet," offering to pay Billy for sexual "favors." What a trap! Porzio was homosexual, using women as a front. Now Helen unknowingly was caught in this web.

And Billy? He was totally confused. Childhood memories resurfaced. The names he had been called as a ten-year-old once again echoed through his ears and into his heart. "Faggot!" "Homo!" Names from the 1950s carried over into the 1970s. So, was he?

An inner battle began to rage in Billy, something that had not happened during his prison experiences. All the time he was in Rikers, he had never thought of looking at another man. He never felt physically or romantically drawn to a man. His prison experiences occurred because other men were drawn to him, initiating advances toward him. It was more of a "prison thing" than a sexual orientation. But his new experiences with Porzio raised deeply uncomfortable questions in him. Was he homosexual? His body had been awakened to something as a child, and he wondered if this was the way he would choose to satisfy his sexual desires as an adult. Why was he constantly being pursued by men? This battle within went on for years. Meanwhile, he continued his relationship not only with Linda but with other women as well.

Billy learned that there was power in knowing Porzio's secret. He took great pleasure in "teasing" him, arousing Porzio's desires. The more Billy taunted and flaunted, the more he gained. In a way, the two were at each other's mercy. Porzio became a slave to Billy's quick wit and lack of fear or inhibition. Billy sensed Porzio's evil nature and hated him for it. At the same time he hated himself for what he did both to Porzio and to himself. Billy's inner struggle was truly an identity crisis. Just who was he, anyway? He felt trapped, and began looking for a way out. Should he move back to New York?

But in New York, another trap was waiting. Billy continued his involvement with Linda Foell, who at age 17 already was using heroin. In the spring of 1970, with her mom on vacation, Linda took advantage of her time alone and staged a party that lasted for eight days. Billy, always ready for a good time, attended. Linda used this opportunity to pressure him to try heroin.

Billy held out. He was deathly afraid of needles. As a 16-year-old, when he saw a nurse approach him with a needle in a hospital emergency room, he had become hysterical, overturning stretchers and upsetting cabinets in order to avoid her needle. Injectable drugs were definitely not his cup of tea. If a drug could be sniffed, snorted, swallowed or smoked, he would try it. But injections were not for Billy!

Linda continued her urging. She was a friend, but Billy worried about her increasing use of heroin. He wanted to prove to her that she could stop. He decided he would use it once, despite his fear of needles, just to show her that it could be done. He hoped that by his example she also would stop. He had been forced to stop using drugs (not that they weren't available) in prison, and knew it was possible.

Once he had agreed to try it, Linda whisked Billy into a walk-in closet. There, in her mother's house, Linda stuck a needle into his upper arm muscle, injecting the worst poison of his life. (Intramuscular drug use is called "skin popping.") And Billy's plan backfired. From that first fix, he was hooked. Billy did not realize that his willpower was no weapon against heroin. His desire for the drug overpowered his fear of needles, and the wish to help Linda become "unhooked" from heroin was gone. He became an expert at finding veins. Why skin pop when you could get the immediate rush of mainlining? The words he had memorized from "King Heroin" were but a faint echo in his mind:

"...you heard my warning and didn't take heed, so put your foot in my stirrup and mount my steed. So ride me, dope fiend, and ride me well, for the white horse of heroin will ride you to hell."

Soon he was injecting not only heroin, but cocaine as well. For the next 17 years, everything he did was geared toward satisfying the urge, the hunger, the tremendous need to fill his body with drugs. The desire for drugs became more important than food, family or freedom. These things often were sacrificed to the god of body pollutants.

After the party ended, Billy went back to New Jersey. Porzio was at that time so intrigued by the hippie movement that it became a ritual for him to drive Billy into the city on weekends, buy a little marijuana for himself, and pick up Linda.

At the same time, Porzio's sexual activity with Billy continued. Eventually Billy told both Helen and Linda about Porzio's secret life. At first neither of them wanted to believe it. But when Porzio began physically and verbally abusing Helen, she began to see that there was another side to him. He was a man without a conscience, using others purely for his own benefit. One day he was your friend; the next, he could knife you in the back.

On Billy's twenty-first birthday Billy's mom found a hypodermic needle among his belongings, and his own secret was out. What could she do – take away his needles? Be angry? Fret? Scold? She believed there was nothing she could do to change the course her son's life was now set on.

About this time, Linda's body gave the first sign of protest against her drug use. Billy began noticing a yellow tint in Linda's eyes, a sure sign of hepatitis. Billy's mother took Linda to New Jersey and placed her under a doctor's care. She stayed in New Jersey for several months, with Helen nursing her back to health.

In July, Billy and Danny drove Bobby to Fort Dix, New Jersey. Billy, deeply addicted to heroin, needed cash. Using the finger-in-the-jacket "I've got a gun" routine, he held up a service station while enroute to Fort Dix. He was caught and sentenced to six months in the penitentiary at Mount Holly, New Jersey.

Billy was paroled in October and went back to Porzio's, this time with Danny. Porzio had a tenant upstairs from whom Billy stole some Seconals. Since it was obvious who was high, it was also clear who had taken the pills. Porzio threw Billy out, putting him on a bus to New York.

Billy had nowhere to go. He slept in Fort Tryon Park and worked as a short-order cook in the cafeteria. It was getting cold, and Linda pleaded with her mom to let Billy stay there. She agreed. In exchange, Billy became a fix-it man for Evelyn. She was happy with this arrangement, and could keep Billy busy since the home lacked a handy man.

At Christmas time, Billy, Linda, Jimmy, and Danny all got temporary jobs at a downtown department store. Billy worked in the men's department. Linda worked as a floating cashier, going from department to department, never totally responsible for a cash register. A New York City female police officer was moonlighting, often working with Linda. She was tipping the till and gave Linda some pointers. Either just take money straight from the till, or watch the customers. Casually walk up to someone with many items and say, "It looks like you have several hundred dollars worth of items there. If you come to my register, I'll ring you up for $50. You give me $75, and no one will be the wiser." Amazingly, Linda was never caught in this deception. She must have been good at sizing up people. And in this way she and Billy supported their habit. Conveniently, a fellow employee also was a heroin dealer, so they had easy access.

Billy lived with Evelyn for three or four months. He found a job at a rental car agency and began looking for a place to live with Linda, finally finding an apartment in the Bronx. Linda was attending the Wilford Academy of Cosmetology. Along with his rent-a-car job, Billy began dealing heroin with "Malibu Benny" (so nicknamed because of the car he drove). Both his and Linda's drug habits increased tremendously during this time. Billy met Frankie and Bonnie, who told him about the Methadone program. Occasionally Frankie would give or sell Methadone to Billy and Linda when they were sick, needing a fix.

One night five or six friends chipped in and bought a half-bundle of heroin. Butchie Link shot up first, and as a practical joke he faked an overdose. He was slapped by a couple guys, and when he "came to" with a dumb smile, everyone chuckled. But the drug really was potent. A couple of other guys got off, then it was Spencer's turn. He sat on a chair in the kitchen and shot up. He never got the needle out of his arm. Being a theatrical actor, no one paid attention to him until he fell off the chair onto the floor, the needle still dangling from his arm. When they realized that this was no act, everyone panicked. Spencer had truly OD'd! They dragged him to the bathtub and dumped him in. They filled the tub with everything cold in the apartment that could be found. Spencer's lips were turning blue, his body lifeless. Billy suddenly noticed that everyone had left except Butch Link and Bobby. Billy said to Bobby,

"What should I do?" Bobby suggested they take Spencer to the roof where he could be found later. "If he dies in your house, you go to jail. If he is found on the roof, who will ever know how he got there?"

Billy couldn't bring himself to do it. He would rather spend time in prison than be in the mental and emotional prison of knowing he had just let Spencer die. Instead, he went to the neighbor's door and banged on it, crying, "Call an ambulance! Someone has OD'd here!" Soon he heard sirens, and both police and ambulance arrived. Billy climbed into the ambulance with Spencer. As they were taking off, he heard the driver say, "It's just another junkie scumbag. Let's take the long way." When they finally got to the hospital, Billy called Spencer's mom, a beautiful Jewish lady. By the time she got there, Spencer had been revived. Billy looked the ambulance driver in the eye and said, "You ——! Tell this lady what you did. She's the mother of that 'scumbag.'" He was furious. Spencer spent several days in the hospital recovering. All the while he was there, he kept asking for Billy, saying, "Thank you, man. You saved my life! You saved my life!"

It was 17 years later that Billy, by then a born-again believer, parked his car on a street in New York and heard a vaguely familiar voice. "Move the car, Schneider! Just move the car!" As Billy looked around, he heard it again. "Do I know you?" he asked the stranger before him. "Do you know me? You saved my life!" And in the middle of the street, Spencer, now a uniformed meter reader, gave Billy a bear hug.

Billy's apartment was under surveillance by the police. One day a knock came on the door. Billy knew there was trouble, because the water had just been shut off, making it impossible to flush drugs down sinks or toilet. This meant one thing – a raid! But Billy, thinking quickly, placed the small amount of heroin he had outside the bathroom window on a ledge. The police never found it. All they found was a few hypodermic needles, and they left thinking they were looking at users, not dealers.

Always in need of extra money, Billy was tempted into trouble on the job. One evening just as he was about to close, a man called, urgently needing a car. "I'll be there in two minutes. Please wait!" Billy did, and for the favor the man gave him a $10 tip. What he didn't mean to do was leave his credit card behind. Billy just looked at this as part of the tip. For a time, Billy felt he was working for "rent-a-card" as he and others used the card. His brother Danny, Linda's brother Jimmy, even Porzio used it before Billy got a call from a credit card detective. "Mr. Schneider," the voice on the phone said, "if you're smart, you will listen. I'll be on the phone for just two minutes. You have the card, we have your signature. There is a balance of $1,768.45 on the card. You have ten days to come up with the money." This shook Billy. He went to his fellow card users, but they all forsook him and fled. With nowhere else to turn, he confessed to Linda's mom, explaining that he had initially used the card to give Linda things he could not afford to buy. Billy hit a soft spot with Evelyn, who wanted the best for her daughter as well. She wrote a check for the entire amount. And although she did it for Billy, her main objective was to spare her own children, both Linda and Jimmy. But Billy lost his job.

Billy's job loss acutely distressed Linda. The apartment was turning into a shooting gallery. Her habit had increased, and she did not think she could survive on what Billy made dealing. She went home to her mom.

Meanwhile, Billy got a job at the Veteran's Administration Hospital as a short-order cook. The job lasted only a short time because Billy was so heavily into drug use.

Billy was tired of the rut. He called his mom in New Jersey. Would she take him in? Yes, she would, so he left his apartment to a friend, Dennis, and in November went back to New Jersey. Here, he could at least decrease his drug use, but he was back in Porzio's sexual trap.

Several months later, Billy was back visiting in the Bronx and ran into Frankie, his old neighbor. Frankie acted friendly, like everything was fine. The next thing Billy knew, sirens were screaming. Frankie had called the police, and Billy was picked up on suspicion of murder. He was taken to the Ogden Avenue Police Station for questioning. It seems Dennis had continued to use his apartment as a shooting gallery. Billy was not sure what happened, but two men had been pushed from his window and were found dead in the alley below. Billy's name was on the lease as legal tenant, so he was under suspicion. The police soon realized that he knew nothing and let him go. But Billy was hurt by Frankie's behavior.

Billy made an application to the Methadone program before he moved to New Jersey. This is a federally funded program, begun experimentally on prisoners at Rikers Island in 1968. Heroin, synthetically produced and labeled "Methadone," is given free of charge to addicts, to be taken orally rather than by injection. Billy's name was placed on a long waiting list that encompassed the entire city. After six weeks, he had heard nothing, so he called again, pleading on the phone. "Look! I'm dying. You want me to die on the streets, is that what you want?" Now he was told to come in. Fresh track marks on top of a prior arrest record for possession of drugs, convinced the officials that Billy was certainly a candidate for the program, and he was accepted the next day, February 2, 1972. He brought Linda with him, and she, too, was placed on Methadone. Once a person is accepted into the program, the spouse or live-in partner would be accepted immediately if also on drugs and seeking help.

Through this program, Billy and Linda were placed on welfare and given subsidized housing and Medicaid, as well as having their drug supplied free. What a deal! Billy no longer would be dependent on Porzio, nor would he have to resort to crime. The program was supposed to move clients toward becoming drug free by gradually reducing the doses of Methadone and at the same time offering counseling, but it rarely functioned that way. Once placed on Methadone, a heroin addict could by his own choice be given Methadone for life. For this reason it is called the Methadone Maintenance program. The purpose, then, seemed to be to reduce crime by giving free drugs rather than helping drug addicts rid themselves of chemical dependence.

Methadone comes in pill form, the pill scored into quarters. When given in the clinic, it was dissolved in juice or water by the nurses, but on Fridays the clients' doses for Saturday and Sunday were given in pill form, making them available on the street, where clients sometimes sold or exchanged them.

Today, 25 years later, Billy Schneider raises this question: "How can a program designed to maintain an addict on a daily basis by administering a Class A narcotic free that person from the power of addiction? It may minimize crime, but it is a crime in and of itself."

While maintaining his addiction by way of the Methadone program, Billy often wondered why he could not shake the urge, the need, the desire to steal. He only recently realized that stealing is a part of the habit. There is more to the god of addiction than filling your body with drugs. Its desire is to bring you down, to make you low, and this god is determined you are to keep your end of the deal. "I... have the power to make a good man evil, and have the power to make a wise man feeble... The life you'll lead will not be nice, you'll beg, borrow and steal just for my price," (from "King Heroin.") That power goes beyond the need to steal for drugs to the addiction of living low itself. The Devil himself wants you to believe that nothing is free, so that when you are offered the free gift of eternal life through Jesus Christ, it is often rejected. When one believes a lie, can the truth make any sense?

The Methadone program with its free synthetic heroin did not stop either Billy or Linda from using other drugs. They became their own chemists, in control of their own altered state of mind. If I want to feel this way, I'll take this. Or if I want to feel that way, I'll take that. Alcohol, pills, cocaine – all could be used along with Methadone to produce the desired effect. And to make matters worse, Billy's counselor in the program was selling him cocaine.

Billy and Linda were brought together by the program. They were told to apply for an apartment in order to take advantage of the subsidized housing. They found a beautiful studio apartment in the Bronx, and Billy once again left New Jersey. He began driving a cab. Because he was on Methadone and working, he saved his first $1,000. Now Billy and Linda really bonded. Together they decorated this apartment, making it home like. They were looking and acting better, both taking better care of themselves. It seemed as though the Methadone program was a good thing. Then Billy had an accident when he drove his cab into a collapsed but unbarricaded and unlit street. He claimed neck and back injuries and received a settlement of $2,500.

With a little money in the bank, Billy and Linda decided to get married. Putting together a "hijack" wedding, they were married on December 2, 1972. Traditional vows were spoken. Perhaps a better rendition would have been "...until confusion do us part." But those vows were spoken before God, and God heard them as they were spoken, "...until death us do part." Billy and Linda had no idea what was in store for them. It did not occur to them that God had his eye on them, as well as on this union they so blithely entered into. Billy had become a husband but had no idea of the responsibility that went with the title.

And it was not long before fighting and physical abuse erupted in the relationship.

CHAPTER 8

Taking
Irresponsibility

After the wedding, Billy and Linda continued to live in their studio apartment for about a year. But, then Porzio came back into the picture, needing help with his business. Billy and Linda packed up and moved into an apartment in Porzio's house in New Jersey. In short order, however, business slowed dramatically, and without work Billy was bored. He had a hard time paying the rent, which Porzio collected by the week. In a month with five weeks, Porzio would ask for an extra week's rent, and he and Billy fought over this. Porzio once again tried his sexual tricks with Billy, but now Billy refused to go for them.

Plagued by a continuing inner battle, Billy decided to put the issue of his sexual orientation to the ultimate test, in the only way he knew how. He would pursue a man himself. He went into a bar purposely to do so. It was easy for him to pick up a male, but immediately he felt filthy. He felt no sense of desire, nor of satisfaction. He did not like what he had done, but finally the question was answered. No, he was not homosexual. The battle regarding his sexual identity was over at last. He did not understand the implications of childhood sexual abuse or the damage it had caused him until much later, when he was able for the first time to talk about the abuse, opening the wounds for true healing. But now he could throw off the doubts those childhood labels had caused him for so many years. And Porzio was no longer a threatening trap.

Billy started his own business, "Mow Joe's Lawn Service." Although he was a terrific advertiser, the business did not go well.

Billy got a break when someone sold him a car for $100, complete with a Pennsylvania license plate good for a year. He applied for a job with a siding company. Going to the manager, he said, "I've never done siding before, but I'm 24 years old, my wife is having a baby, and I need a job. If you show me once, I will know how to do it." The boss liked his attitude and hired him. He was true to his word – he learned after being shown only once, and quickly became an expert siding mechanic.

Billy had stopped using Methadone when they moved to New Jersey. It was just too far to travel into New York City. He thought Linda had quit the drug as well. Billy substituted alcohol for other drugs, believing it to be a better choice. He fell for the argument that alcohol is not a drug, in large part because alcohol is "legal." Even rehab programs speak of alcohol and drug abuse as if they are two different things. If people understood that a drug is a drug is a drug, and that this includes alcohol and cigarettes, perhaps governments would make both alcohol and cigarettes illegal along with other drugs. It is a double standard. And, in truth, alcohol is a more dangerous drug than most, the withdrawal more painful. It is the drug that is more responsible for the spread of AIDS than any other substance. Why? Under the influence of alcohol, people are inclined to try things that they wouldn't do if sober – often with no memory of what they have done. Alcohol played havoc with Billy's daily activities. He frequently stayed out all night in bars, which caused him to miss work often.

Billy and Linda's baby was due in June. When Linda went into labor, Billy brought her into New York, accompanied by his brother Bobby. At about 2 a.m. they dropped her off, then went to a local bar to wait for the birth. When the bar closed at 4 a.m., they returned to the hospital to the news that William James Schneider had been born at 3:05 a.m., June 7, 1974. Peering at his new son, Billy thought, "He doesn't look a bit like me." He felt no sense of bonding to this tiny person, who from the moment of birth had his own set of struggles. Alone in an isolette, he was withdrawing from Methadone with the help of Phenobarbital. Once again the generational torch was passed. With his parents steeped in the hippie era and strung out on drugs, little Billy had to make it on his own, even in the crib.

A fellow siding mechanic told Billy of a place for rent, an old barn converted into a house. The landlady was about 85 years old, and she agreed to let Billy rent it for $175 per month. This would free Billy from Porzio. The place needed major repairs, and Billy was willing to do the work. Linda wept when she saw it, but by December it was a cozy home, and Linda thought it was the best place in which she had lived.

But a new home did not solve all the problems in the Schneider household. Adding to an already stressed relationship, Billy invited his friend Ricky to move in because of difficulty in his own marriage. Billy spent more time with Ricky than he did with Linda, shooting pool and going to bars. When Ricky joined the Navy at Christmas time, it seemed as though things might improve.

But in February, Billy came home early one day during a rainstorm. He saw that the inside door had blown open, and as he approached the house he could see little Billy inside, grinning at him from his crib. He stopped to greet him and called out for Linda. There was no answer. Where was she? How was it that the baby, now eight months old, was home alone? Billy was alarmed, thinking perhaps Linda had gone around the block to a local store and had run into trouble. It never occurred to him what was really going on. He waited for hours, with no way to figure out where she was.

Eight hours passed before Linda returned home. As Billy saw her car pull up and watched her get out, his senses sharpened. Something looked all too familiar about her demeanor. "No! NO!" he cried as she came in the door.

"No, what?" Linda asked.

"Give me the keys," Billy demanded. Going to the car, he found it open, but the glove compartment was locked. Sure enough, inside the glove compartment were two bottles of Methadone, marked "Linda Foell." In his fury, he took the drug and dumped it down the drain. Now she was furious, and frantic as well, as she watched her god wash down the kitchen sink.

Without Billy's knowledge, Linda had continued taking Methadone. This meant trips to New York City three times a week (Methadone was then being distributed Monday, Wednesday and Friday). Sometimes she took little Billy with her, but more often it seemed easier to her to leave him home alone. Her intention was to get the Methadone and return home immediately. Even this would mean leaving him for long periods of time. But she often would become distracted doing other things, completely forgetting her responsibilities as a mother.

In her addicted state, Linda also told Billy that she was taking little Billy to the baby clinic for check-ups. She would make up stories of his progress, even reporting his increasing weights. In reality, if she took little Billy out it was to go with her to pick up her Methadone, and she never took him for checkups.

One day Evelyn stopped by and found baby Billy in his crib, soaking wet, but with a huge smile for Grandma. Grandma cleaned him up and fed him, then waited for Linda to return. This did not happen for hours. Her relationship with Linda was so strained and fragile that she did not dare to do what she should have done. She feared that taking her grandson home with her or getting social services involved could snap the very thin line of communication she and Linda already had. She did not understand this world of drugs and free love in which her daughter lived.

Helen was aware as well of the dynamics of parenting in this household. She would sometimes have little Billy stay with her. But the truth was that the little boy was abandoned by his mother and no one stepped in. Linda would excuse herself by saying, "I'm just not cut out to be a mother."

Adding to Billy's frustration with marriage and parenting was the fact that Linda cultivated relationships with other men, even in their own home. The latest was Hank. When Billy realized this, he gave her an ultimatum: "Either get rid of Hank, or pack your bags." She chose to pack her bags, leaving her husband and eight-month-old son. For her, it was a matter of survival, and she needed to take care of herself. Plainly it was not possible to be both mom and drug addict.

Now the job of parenting fell on Billy. He took this as seriously as he could, feeding little Billy a balanced diet and clearing up a terrible diaper rash. By this time Billy was working at a new job. His new boss, Dick, had a large family, including several beautiful daughters. Everyone in this family was doing drugs. He and his wife were separated, the wife living with another man whom Dick hired as a way of helping to support his own children who were living with their mother. This confusing picture was just a "normal" part of Billy's life. Two of Dick's daughters began to share the job of baby-sitting Billy Jr. so they could chase after Billy. Then Billy met Dick's oldest daughter, Terri. A beautiful 17-year-old, she was mesmerized by Billy. Captivated by his sensitive nature, she fell in love with Billy. It was the beginning of a seven year relationship.

Billy's life became even more complicated as he juggled parenting, work, and the pursuit of a new relationship. Alcohol continued to take a toll on his life as well. He tried leaving little Billy with Terri's mother so he and Terri could spend time together. Her house, however, was dirty and smelly, and Billy did not think it a safe environment for a baby, especially with sewer and water problems added to poor housekeeping.

After about three months he had enough. He dressed his son, put him in the car, and, with Terri, set off to find his wife. She had by now left her boyfriend Hank and moved to New York with her brother Jimmy. When he got into the city, Billy called her, and she said, "We're just leaving to see a movie." Well, Billy wasn't going to let that put him off, so he cruised around until he found Jimmy and Linda in line at the Fordham Road Theater. He got out of the car and placed their son, not yet one year old, in Linda's arms. "Here, you take him. I can't take it any more." And with that he drove off, abandoning little Billy in no better circumstances than the boy's mother had a few months earlier.

It was Uncle Jimmy who finally took over the job of bringing up little Billy. He and Linda were both heavily into drugs. There was not much joy in life for either of them, but Jimmy was the family brain. He saw the value of education, and, in spite of being deep into the New York City drug scene of the 1970s, had gotten some education beyond high school. Jimmy's father had been working on getting his son into West Point, and Jimmy might have made it had it not been for his father's untimely death. Jimmy read to little Billy and taught him his numbers, letters, colors. And later, it was Jimmy who helped him with his school work.

Billy began living with Terri. She already had been exposed to drugs, right in her father's house. One night, as if by mutual consent, they both decided to do some dope. It did not take long to find a source of heroin, and Billy was once again into the world of needles. Soon both of them were heavily into IV drugs.

Billy felt little concern for Linda and visited his son only sporadically. When he did visit, he usually was high, the drugs changing him from a sweet, fun-loving guy into an irritable, hostile person. It was a dark time for everyone, with each person desperate to take care of their own needs, trying in vain to feel good.

Both Billy and Linda tried to fool themselves into thinking they were happy living their separate lives. It was, after all, the era of free love, where everything was beautiful in its own way. Drugs were cool, and wasn't doing your own thing the most important principle to follow? What Billy did not hear from Linda was her inner rage toward him that had built up through the years, even to the point of devising a plan to murder him. And what Linda did not hear from Billy was his desperation with the endless traps of his life. She did not hear that Billy felt the jaws of these traps getting ready to snap shut on him. The atmosphere in which they lived never allowed either of them to express their true feelings, and Billy thought that Linda was perfectly content that his life did not include her.

Linda's expectations from life certainly were not being realized. In her early teens, when she first began experimenting with drugs in order to fit in with her peers, she had no idea that drugs would interfere with her entire life. She did not think, as she took her first hit of heroin, that she would become its slave. Instead of fulfilled dreams, her life became a cycle of pain, denial of the pain, cover-up with drugs, and guilt. Neither Billy nor Linda had any idea that there was an answer to be found, that there was a way out of the web they were caught in. Nothing – not sex, drugs, or even trying to do right – was ultimately fulfilling.

Billy and Terri moved to New York in order to be close to the Methadone program. Billy was out of work, and getting back into the program meant welfare. The two of them lived here and there, sometimes with friends. Billy, as always, was clever, coming up with some way to make money. While he was once again on Methadone, he was still buying cocaine, and sometimes heroin. He was staying away from stealing, but his life was in a downward spiral. He did not have his own home; he was sleeping with other women besides his girlfriend; and, he was not working.

The Methadone program was not a way out of either drugs or trouble. Twice Billy witnessed violence at the program. One day, on the steps outside the program, a friend was shot and killed in front of Terri. Clients in the program were protected from the law. Even if they were known dealers they could not be turned in. Billy presumed that it was the FBI who had done the killing. Earlier, as Billy waited in line for his weekend doses, four armed men entered the building. Linda had just been served and was waiting for Billy in a nearby cafe. These violent and foul-mouthed men made off with backpacks full of the Methadone.

Those who know Billy now have a hard time imagining him so enslaved to something that he stood brainlessly in line waiting for his next fix. It is much easier to imagine him on the streets finding his own means of survival.

It was against this backdrop of desperation that Billy, on March 11, 1977, climbed to the top of the George Washington Bridge in hopes of being heard. He and Terri were living in a rooming house in Manhattan. Billy used to steal food from the refrigerator. He found that he was stealing from a young man named Rene. Rene was a new Christian who was living in the rooming house temporarily. After Rene's salvation, his pastor had urged him to move out of the situation he was in, living with his girlfriend and her three children. He now was waiting to marry her.

On hearing some of Billy's stories, Rene said, "You remind me of my pastor. I wish you could meet him. He used to be into drugs like you are." He brought his Bible during one of these visits and showed Billy a tract written by his pastor, Tom Mahairas. Tom! Billy's childhood friend and later his drug partner. The person who had already confronted Billy with the offer of God's forgiveness. "Jesus loves you!" he would say to Billy. "Yeah? So does my old lady!" Billy would scornfully reply, referring to his girlfriend. Now, here was another brush with real life, but Billy turned a deaf ear. Instead, he made a desperate attempt to be heard by climbing the bridge. The gesture did nothing to change his life, and he ended up back in the rooming house with Terri.

CHAPTER 9

Trying to Make it Right

Now, Billy thought, there was no way out. In the most dramatic way he could think of, he had tried to ask for help, but it failed. The result of this failure was a hopelessness that shrouded Billy's life, in spite of the fact that marriage and fatherhood made him act a bit more responsibly. For four years he had not been arrested. He was generally maintaining a steady job during that time, giving him a semblance of respectability. But this was not enough to help him see a way out of the trap of drugs and sex.

Billy's attitude about himself showed in his arrest record, which, starting in 1977, began to mount. He continued living with Terri, but, as his criminal activity increased, her interest waned. The two of them moved back to New Jersey where she began working as a go-go dancer. This did not help the relationship. Billy worked periodically during this time. Drugs continued to be central to both of them.

In spite of the darkness in his life, Billy had a God-consciousness deep inside. Raised as a Roman Catholic, his father's religion, he made claims to knowing God. He often had time for introspection as he sat in prison. Each time he was released, his intention was to live productively, to not use drugs, to work and stay out of trouble. But each time, usually within hours, he was right back in the same old rut.

When the world couldn't help him, Billy visited the Manhattan Bible Church with Terri. Hearing the gospel, they both raised their hands for salvation. Were they truly born again that day? They went their way, their lives unchanged, and did not return to church. Whether or not he was offered discipleship is unclear, but Billy was not nurtured as a new Christian. He did not truly understand salvation, nor was he clearly convicted of the gross sin in which he lived.

In 1979, still with Terri, Billy found a privately run Methadone program called "MAP," standing for "Methadone Abstinence Program." This program was staffed by college students who never had been on drugs. The idea and atmosphere here was different from other Methadone programs. This was a place for the addict who was serious about stopping drug use, including Methadone. No one was given maintenance doses. Rather, doses were gradually decreased in a plan set up by client and counselor until the client was free of the drug. Billy and Terri made a determined effort to stop the Methadone madness.

Billy decided April 17 would be his last day on Methadone. His friend Ricky, who had just been released from the Navy, called him from Florida and invited him down. They could stay in his mother's bungalow in West Palm Beach. Billy decided this would be an ideal way to complete his withdrawal from Methadone, so, with Phenergan from a doctor to help him, he boarded a plane for the first time. He did indeed get off Methadone. After two weeks, he returned to New Jersey.

In early June, Billy and Terri decided to return to Florida for a vacation together, and, since he was "between" jobs, he went ahead of her. Billy and Ricky floated in the beautiful Florida water. Billy pretended to be drowning, wondering what it would be like. At the same time, back in New York, Billy's father truly was drowning.

On a Friday afternoon, Sonny Schneider had left a bar with friend Joe Thompson, headed for the Hudson River. On Monday morning, Joe's body was found washed ashore. Someone told Bobby, who went to the waterfront. He was frantic, saying, "My dad was with Joe!" With Bobby watching, they dragged the river for Sonny, and sure enough, found his body. It was horrifying for Bobby to see the body of his father, now bloated and ghastly, with one eye open, one eye shut. Helen called Billy in Florida, and he came home for the funeral, but his mom did not attend.

What went through Billy's mind? The lyrics of the song, "In the Living Years," made him think of all the things he could have told his father – and all the things he wished he heard from him. He did not grieve that his dad was dead. His relationship with him had been negative. And yet, even then, Billy thought that he could have shared the gospel with him – the gospel he had recently raised his hand to accept. Yes, Billy had heard the gospel. But he did not know Jesus.

On his return from Florida, Billy got a job with a cable TV company, and he and Ricky began selling cocaine. Soon Billy was again injecting both cocaine and heroin. By November of 1979 he was again on

Methadone. He had returned to his life of crime, drugs, and women.

Almost by accident Billy found a source of counterfeit money when Terri's aunt was in financial trouble. She and her husband had split, and her husband had left a collection of guns behind, intending to return for them. Billy offered to get rid of them for her. He took several rifles in the trunk of his car and headed for the city.

He went to see Gabe, who was in the Mafia and who had been a source of cocaine for him. Gabe had taken a liking to Billy, feeling he could trust him. He had once gone out of his way to make someone stop harassing Billy. Gabe had been responsible for killing people, so his threats were taken seriously. Billy showed Gabe the rifles, and someone pressed a stack of $50 bills in his hand in exchange for them. Counterfeit! But they looked so good even the banks had trouble spotting them. Billy received a short course in the use of counterfeit money that night – where to pass them and where not to, and how to make them look aged. His share of the $5,000 he received for the rifles was soon spent.

When Porzio heard of the counterfeit money, he struck up a relationship with Gabe. Porzio was deeply in debt and began making deals for counterfeit.

One evening Billy came around to Gabe's with some money for cocaine. As he went into Gabe's building he saw two guys hanging around outside. At first, Billy didn't pay attention, but as he came inside, there was a third one on the stairway. He stopped Billy, asking "You going to apartment 2-E?"

"Why ya' asking me? You the landlord, trying to collect the rent?" Billy was flippant with him, but as quickly and as unobtrusively as possible he made his way out of the building and headed to the bar where he knew Gabe hung out. He saw Gabe leave the bar, and, being cautious not to get too close, he said, "Gabe, I think I'm being followed. Narcs are at your house." He then continued walking in a different direction than Gabe. Moments later, as Billy watched, Gabe was picked up. Little did Billy know that Porzio was in the car, a bag over his head. He used Gabe, then turned him in. Billy was never sure why Porzio did this. Was it purely out of malice? Or had Porzio, in order to impress his family, reported Gabe to his brother-in-law, who was in the FBI? Or, had he been caught and made a deal to save his own skin?

Meanwhile, danger still lurked for Billy. He was in a bad spot, but he was not aware just how bad. He had unknowingly led the narcotics agents to Gabe, but it appeared to Gabe's bodyguard that Billy was a part of the set-up.

Billy made his way back to the bar and met up with Terri. Moments later, Gabe's bodyguard Raymond walked into the bar and asked Billy to step outside. Billy did so, and on the curb was a waiting car. Raymond shoved Billy inside. Poor Terri! Having been traumatized earlier by Billy's bridge climb, she was frantic once again. "Don't hurt him! Please don't hurt him!" she screamed helplessly as the car sped away.

Billy was taken to the river. With loaded gun in hand, Raymond said to him, "I hate to do this to you, but I'm going to have to kill you. You set Gabe up." Raymond had witnessed Billy's short exchange with Gabe just before Gabe had been picked up. It certainly looked as though Billy had been leading the narcs to him.

Billy, knowing his own innocence, kept his cool. He reasoned with Raymond: "Look at it this way, Raymond. You know I wouldn't do a thing to hurt Gabe. You know we've been friends a long time. Gabe is with the narcs right now, and they can't hold him for more than seventy-two hours. Let's wait until he's out. Ask him. If I did set him up, you can kill me then. You know I couldn't get away too far."

Raymond was raving, high on cocaine, and would have killed Billy. But the driver calmed him down, urging him to reckon with what Billy had said. After all, what if they did kill an innocent man? Gabe would not be pleased. This could put them in jeopardy, for they both knew that Gabe liked Billy.

Billy's quick thinking, his calm demeanor in the face of danger, and his way with words saved his life that night. Thankfully, Raymond did not know at that moment that it was Porzio who had set Gabe up. Otherwise, the picture would have looked even more suspicious for Billy, and it might have been impossible to convince Raymond of Billy's innocence.

Raymond let Billy out of the car. Later, when Gabe was released and heard the story, he gave Billy a big hug. "Of course I know you were innocent!"

This incident completely severed any remaining relationship between Porzio and Billy. Helen had left him and returned to New York. It was not long afterward that Porzio was found dead in his bathtub, apparently from a heart attack.

By the early 1980s, there had been much stress and strain on the relationship between Billy and Terri. She was fed up with his frequent trips to prison, his relationships with other women, his heavy drug use. She needed a more stable life, and, although she truly loved Billy, she left him. She had gradually withdrawn from Billy, seeing other men and making her own way with her job as a go-go dancer.

Billy did not want to let her go. Their relationship was the most stable one Billy ever had. Terri truly loved Billy, and in the best way she knew, tried to help him do right. But she was not equipped to change his life, being heavily into drugs and sex herself. And Billy's personality was strong. He was much more a leader than she, so in reality, where he went, she had followed. And where he was going was not good. Finally, she could only help herself, and the best way to do that was to get out.

Billy was alone. He may have been lonely in the past, but he had had an attachment with Linda Foell, a relationship that led eventually to marriage. Then there were seven or eight years with Terri. Life was different now. He found himself sinking in muck and mire, his life becoming a roller-coaster of drugs, sex, shoplifting, and prison. Cocaine was perhaps the one thing that fulfilled his desire for companionship. It all added up to emptiness.

CHAPTER 10

Supporting
a Habit

After he and Terri split up, Billy's life spun into confusion. Billy had learned from Uncle Sonny the art of crime, but he refined that art. He became a master thief, a criminal motivated by the thrill of being able to pull off a theft. His crimes never were violent; rather, they were an exercise of the mind, a response to an inner dare as well as a fulfillment of the need for drug money. And, if you didn't get caught, Billy believed, it wasn't wrong.

His arrest record began to mount. In New Jersey alone, Billy was arrested 21 times and was sentenced to prison nine times. Most of his convictions were for possession of stolen property or vehicles, shoplifting, larceny, or possession of narcotics or narcotic equipment. He used eight aliases and three Social Security numbers.

Then there is his New York arrest record, spanning the 20 years from 1966 to 1986. In spite of the number of arrests, he got away with years of shoplifting, stealing, drug dealing, and passing counterfeit money. He was guilty of far more than he was prosecuted for.

If crime were funny, Billy could tell funny stories. Using his considerable wit all too often for criminal purposes, he found that crime does – and does not – pay. What he didn't take into consideration at the time was this: "Sin always takes you farther than you want to go, keeps you longer than you want to stay, costs you more than you intend to pay." It is all too clear that Billy now is paying a terrible price for his crimes. Crime is not funny, and the price is not right.

This story could be titled "The short happy life of your stolen car." Billy was driving a stolen van when it broke down in front of a high-class restaurant. Next to it was a heliport. A helicopter landed as Billy was standing there trying to decide what to do. Billy felt something strike his chest as the wind from the chopper blades stirred up the dust. As it fell to the ground, Billy saw it was a $50 bill! He put his foot on it, noticing at the same time two men running toward him. Were they chasing the money? No; they wanted Billy to move his van. "No problem," Billy said, "except that it broke down, and I need to make a phone call." It would seem "luck" was with Billy on this day. Fifty dollars richer, he walked toward the restaurant. As he observed the attendants parking cars, he saw them park a 450 SL Mercedes, and took note of where they placed the keys. The attendants both left to park other cars and Billy walked into their booth, picked up the keys and drove off with his new car. Checking around as he drove he found the car was registered to "Commissioner – New York State Police." What a surprise awaited the commissioner later! In the glove compartment were easy-to-sell bridge booklets, worth at least $120 on the street. Then there was a cache of rolled up change and a handful of bridge tokens, also an easy sell at $1 to $2 apiece.

On his way home to Newark, Billy copped drugs – coke and Methadone. He shot up at home, then returned to the city's drug area to purchase more drugs. A neighborhood punk walked by and warned him, "Sucker, this ain't your car! The police are just around the corner!"

Billy exited the car just in time and walked nonchalantly into the building. The police eyed the car, not suspecting it was stolen. It certainly smacked of a drug dealer's wheels to them. Billy, curious and brazen, came out of the building. The police put him up against their cruiser to search him, along with another person. As they were searching the other person first, Billy edged the key out of his pocket and dropped it on the rear bumper of the police car. When he was searched, his drugs and syringes were found and confiscated. The police were no wiser.

Someone else told the police, "The guy who drove up in this car is a big dealer. He's inside the building." The police fell for this story and began to go inside. But on second thought, one of them went back to his car, opened the trunk and took out a huge blade. He used this to slash all four tires on the Mercedes. As soon as they were inside, Billy retrieved the key from the rear bumper of the cruiser, which the officer had overlooked in opening the trunk. He went to the trunk of the Mercedes, took out the clothes he had stashed there, and made his way home. The next day, Billy returned to the scene of the crime and found the Mercedes completely stripped.

Another time, on the prowl in Newark, he found an unlocked car. On the dashboard he saw some nice leather gloves. Inside the car he looked around to see what else he might find. The glove compartment yielded only a pair of sunglasses, not much of a commodity in the winter. He peered into the back seat, and spotted a neatly folded Newark police officer's uniform. Now this was a find, and his for the taking.

The next day, he ripped off a sewing kit and went to work shortening the pants. With the uniform trimmed to fit, he put on shirt, tie, pants, jacket and hat. He boarded a bus, casually flashed his wallet open and the driver waved him to a seat. He went to the Willowbrook Shopping Mall in Wayne, New Jersey. Entering a department store, he went in search of stereos. No one was around. He unpacked a portable radio, a "boom box" with detachable speakers, which in those days sold for over $500. He placed the instructions inside his shirt, attached the speakers, and walked out of the store. No one attempted to stop him. He walked out of the mall. Now he had a problem. He could not sell a radio to a drug dealer while dressed as a policeman. He needed a phone booth in which to do a Superman act. But, another small problem. All he had was the uniform. So he again boarded a bus free of charge, using the same wallet-flashing technique. Still no one looked at him suspiciously, even though he was now carrying a large radio. He went home, changed clothes, and sold the radio for $100. Aware that impersonating a police officer was dangerous business, he threw the uniform away.

On another occasion, he was in a barber shop. A police officer was getting a haircut and a shave, and while he was in the barber chair, Billy neatly took the badge off the hat the officer had hung on the rack. He used this as a scare tactic to steal drugs. He would watch someone make a deal, then walk up to them and flash the badge. "Gimme the dope you just bought. I need it for a plant." Or, "Either you give me the drugs or I'll lock you up." Often police would hang around dope dealers impersonating buyers in order to make arrests. It was impossible to tell them from the real street people, the real buyers. They would dress in filthy clothes, with unshaven faces and long hair. In this way, Billy got a lot of drugs. Someone who had just bought drugs did not want to mess with the law; they'd much rather just give up what they had.

Billy enjoyed getting into the policeman act. Following a drunk driver gave him an idea. Acting as though he were talking on a radio, but using only a cigarette box, he pulled out alongside the car and waved the driver over. When the driver complied, Billy made him get out of the driver's seat and into the back of the car. "Hand me your wallet!" Billy ordered. Several people were talking on a nearby porch. "That's the police!" he heard them saying. With the man's wallet in hand, Billy jumped back into his own car and drove away.

"Sometimes I wouldn't even think," Billy remembers. "The idea would just come." Billy was bold, and very good at being very bad!

One day he was in a bookstore and saw someone looking at a book that sold for about $80. This was not a small book. Billy saw the man was thinking of buying it, so he sidled up to him and asked, "You want that book? Meet me outside and I'll give it to you for $50." The man agreed. Billy stuck the book down his pants. Then he picked up another book and walked casually out of the store. The alarm went off, and Billy, remaining just outside the door, said to the manager who came scurrying, "Hey, I just wanted to see if it worked!" and handed the book in his hands back. Not another question was asked, and Billy walked off. He pulled the other book out of his pants and made an easy $50. (Billy got this idea from a movie, to the shameful "credit" of Hollywood.)

Billy even ripped off a keyboard with remarkable ease. He wore loose pants and a large coat. Stuffing the keyboard into his pants, he tightened the belt. The keyboard tickled his chin, but no one noticed.

Billy was in a clothing store one day and decided to steal a leather jacket. Using a tool, he removed the anti-theft device. Dropping this device into the pocket of an innocent woman shopper, he then waited for her to exit the store. When she did, the alarm went off and security hustled out of the store after her. Watching calmly as they brought the unsuspecting and now upset woman back into the store, Billy walked out with the jacket when they disappeared with her into a back office.

Billy had a friend named Danny, a 62-year-old heroin addict. For a time Billy lived with him. One morning, Danny woke him up and said, "Hey, kid, I know where we can get razor blades. I know someone who'll gimme two bucks a pack." Billy thought Danny was crazy and didn't go. Billy was sick anyway, needing a fix. About an hour later, Danny came back. He had lifted fifteen packs of razor blades, gotten $30, and brought heroin home with him. Danny could never locate a vein, so he gave Billy a fix in exchange for Billy injecting him. In this way, Billy and Danny would feed off each other, one getting the heroin, the other administering it.

It caused Billy to rethink the razor blade idea. This would become his biggest scam ever. In the beginning, he would walk in a store with a bag of dirty laundry, making sure stinky socks and underwear were at the top. He would fill the bag with razor blades, then buy a small box of soap, to do his laundry, of course.

One day Billy was in a store and saw a lady with a box of disposable diapers. That box is huge, Billy noted to himself. At the same time an idea hatched in his mind. He went to the baby department, carefully opened a box of diapers, and emptied it, hiding the diapers here and there on the shelf. Then he took this box to the razor blade department and filled it. Carefully he taped the box shut and replaced it on the shelf, placing it behind other boxes. Now, he picked up another box of diapers and bought it. He made sure that he picked up the opposite kind (daytime instead of nighttime) from the box he had just filled. After he left the store, he waited a few minutes, then returned. He found the same cashier and said to her, "Oh, dear! I got the wrong kind of diapers! But what do I know?" She did just what she was supposed to. She waved him on to go pick up the right kind. He left his purchase with her and retrieved the box filled with razor blades. The cashier innocently waved him out the door with his haul.

Billy had heard of an outlet for the razor blades, a drug store in New York City. The only difference between this store and any other one was that most of its items for sale had been shoplifted. The manager was a crafty fellow. He would accept any over-the-counter items and pay one-third the retail.

Going into the drug store, Billy indicated to the manager, sitting in his office with a large glass window, that he wanted to come up. Seeing the diaper box in Billy's hand, he shooed him away disgustedly, indicating with his gestures, "I don't need diapers!"

"No, no! I gotta talk to you!" Reluctantly, the manager came down. "I got razor blades," Billy said. Then, he brought Billy up, and Billy walked out with $700. No wonder he believed crime paid!

After that he was a regular in the little glass office. The manager was intrigued. He said to Billy one day, "I thought you were a little jerk when I first saw you with that diaper box. But you're the best." And he was. No one else even came close. He was so good he even stole from the manager. Once he came in with only five packs of razor blades. The manager had stacks of boxes of razor blades in his office, many from Billy. As the manager was busy with something else, Billy shoved handfuls of razors from these boxes into his duffel bag and resold them to him, walking out with $250.

Once Billy was picked up by the police with friends Richie and Donna. They all had been shoplifting, and Richie was followed into the parking lot and arrested in the car. Billy and Donna were released since nothing was found on them. Richie was fuming, knowing there were diaper boxes of razors in the trunk which the police never investigated. The irony is that Billy and Donna went right out shoplifting again and this time they, too, were caught, and all three spent 30 days in the county jail.

Billy had members of the Mafia approach him when they realized how clever he was and how completely unafraid he was of doing the things he did. The absence of fear was the key to his "success" as a criminal. He never was violent and never harmed anyone. Billy was charged several times with resisting arrest, as well as for fighting, but never in connection with a theft. Once he stole a Mafia kingpin's car. It was old and easy to jump-start. Billy was arrested, but when the kingpin realized who the thief was, he went with Billy to court to drop the charges. As they were getting ready to walk out, the judge said, "That'll be $50 to cover court costs," which the kingpin paid.

Outside the courtroom, Billy asked him, "How about $25 for a little food and a fix?" He was sick, in need of heroin. The man gave him this, too. His Mafia friends liked him; they liked how his mind worked, liked how he could always get them good stuff, but they did not like that he was using heroin. "Why do you ruin yourself with that junk?" they would ask him.

Once he walked into a store with Donna. At the entrance was a shopping cart filled with razor blades ready to be stocked in the checkout lanes. What a find! "Donna, you gotta help me. You create a disturbance. Fake fainting." She did, and store personnel came running. "Call an ambulance!" "Get the emergency kit!" While all eyes were focused on this scene, Billy walked out pushing the cart. He packed his trunk with razor blades, then waited, and waited, and waited for Donna. To his way of thinking, it took her far too long to convince them that she was really okay. But for this heist he made over $2,000.

Over and over, Billy continually hit the same chain of stores for his razor blade heists. Their supplier realized that razor blades had become a huge loss item for the chain, and wanted to find the problem. Not only was Billy lifting them, but another male/female team cloned what Billy did. The stores could not figure out his MO (modus operandi).

Finally they caught Billy on camera, and he was arrested in West Orange. As Billy was being charged with shoplifting, he heard an officer coming down the hall to put him in his cell. But wait! Someone wanted to see him! The security person from the supply house came into the room like a raging bull. "Do you realize these stores have lost over $500,000 in razor blades in the past year and a half?" He wanted to see to it that Billy got the maximum sentence, and lay on a load of guilt. Sad to say, instilling guilt was not possible. By this time Billy was stealing nothing but razor blades. It had become big time business for him. His sentence? Only nine months in the Essex County Jail.

But when you have nothing to lose, what does it matter if you get caught? Billy had no reputation, except as a good thief. He had no worldly goods to call his own, he held on to relationships loosely. In his circumstances he could afford to be bold.

A truly bold move was stealing a garbage truck from a Mafia-run carting company and driving it to the Essex County Jail. It happened this way: Billy was spending one of many nights on the street. It was cold and windy, and he needed a warm spot to park himself, just to think for a few minutes. Walking along Bloomfield Avenue in Newark, he came upon three or four garbage trucks, and decided to check them out. A careless person had left keys in the ignition of one of them. He jumped in and started the truck just to get warm. Around 11 p.m., he got out and called his friend Donna. "I just got my welfare check today," she said. But she needed transportation to cash it. Also, she wanted to bail her husband Richie out of jail the next morning as he had been incarcerated for shoplifting.

"I'll pick you up," said Billy.

"What will you be driving?" Donna asked.

"You'll see when I get there!" Billy replied.

Billy drove across town and parked in front of Donna's house. He slept in the truck, and in the morning after Donna's mother left for work, Billy honked the horn. Donna came out and jumped in the garbage truck. They laughed all the way to jail. Parking two blocks away from the jail, they bailed Richie out and started toward the garbage truck. When he saw what they were going to get into, he went wild. But he was so sick from withdrawal that it really didn't matter too much, and he slept as they drove all the way to New York City's lower east side in the garbage truck. Here they found heroin. It was a great spot to get high, since no one could see them in the truck.

They spent the day in the city shooting heroin and cocaine before heading back to New Jersey. In Newark, Billy left the garbage truck with Richie and Donna. And what became of the truck? Who knows? Like having an elephant in the back yard, who would notice a thing like that?

When Donna and Richie's marriage broke up, Billy went to California with Donna, both of them thinking they could start over. Billy's brother Danny was in Los Angeles, and Billy and Donna visited him. Danny had hooked up with a wealthy woman, and married her. He was living like a king, but was unwilling to share the spoils with his brother. Instead, he sent him off to some of his drug-using acquaintances. The change of geography did nothing to improve Billy's circumstances, and soon after his arrival in Los Angeles he found a source of heroin, shooting up with borrowed and dirty needles.

He and Donna went shopping one day with their new friends, when Billy decided to do a little nosing around. He walked into the storeroom of a large department store and found a stairway leading directly to the roof. There seemed to be no alarm system attached to this exit, so Billy left it unlatched from the inside. Casually leaving the storeroom, Billy was devising a plan. He would return later that night, climb to the rooftop, and, in reverse Santa mode, leave with merchandise. His new friend John agreed to go with him in exchange for some of the goods. He was to be the parking lot watchdog while Billy went in.

All they needed was a short ladder for Billy to be able to go from entrance overhang to roof with ease. And sure enough, the rooftop door had not been locked. Billy went in and filled two duffel bags with electronic equipment, watches, radios, and cameras. A dumpster filled with cardboard packing was sitting right next to the building. Billy dropped the duffel bags into the dumpster and came down. However, John, the point man, had chickened out and was nowhere to be found. Pretty soon he came walking up, but Billy was furious with John for not keeping his end of the deal, so he gave him only a radio. He kept the rest of the loot for himself, which he sold for drugs. Billy always could make a sale.

California did not offer a new and healthy life for Billy. He had been hopeful about his connection with Danny and his new-found wealth, but that fantasy was short-lived. With nothing for him in the West, Billy made his way back to New Jersey.

In his downward spiral, Billy's arrest record began to look like this:

12/4/82, arrested; possession stolen property, narcotic
    equipment, possession.
12/15/82, arrested; possession stolen vehicle, possession
    stolen property.
1/27/83, arrested; burglary.
2/2/83, arrested; possession stolen property, making
    false report.
2/4/83, arrested; shoplifting.
2/27/83, arrested; shoplifting.
3/10/83, arrested; shoplifting.
4/16/83, arrested; receiving stolen property, larceny,
    dangerous drugs, narcotic equipment, possession.
5/12/83, arrested; receiving stolen vehicle.
5/26/83, arrested; shoplifting.
6/9/83, arrested; shoplifting, possession stolen property.

In the end, Billy's record mounted to 39 arrests. Although one might look upon that as a string of failures for a thief, sometimes an arrest was worthwhile, even planned, as it allowed the person to be under shelter, with a bed, food and shower.

But Billy, a very good thief, was coming unraveled. By this time, he had spent a total of several years in various prisons and jails, not including his time at Rikers Island in the 1960s. But far too often he was arrested and let go with only a suspended sentence or fine. Now his messy life was catching up with him, and in 1983 he was given an aggregate sentence to the New Jersey State Penitentiary for four years.

CHAPTER 11

The State Penitentiary

W hen Billy entered Leesburg State Prison in 1983, he was desperate and despondent. He did want to change, but everything he tried had failed. In spite of being classified "4-F" in 1966, deemed unfit for armed services duty because of drug addiction, he never was offered rehabilitation. He had been in and out of jails and prison ever since, drugs in control of his life. Pondering all this, he felt his sentence was unjust and inhumane. He petitioned the New Jersey Supreme Court and applied for a change of venue in order to be placed in drug rehab. At last, Billy was heard; he was released from prison and placed on one year's probation. The terms of probation required that he spend one year in an in-house drug rehabilitation center. If he violated probation, he then would be returned to the penitentiary for the entire four-year sentence.

After serving a year, Billy left prison and went to the Institute of Human Development in Atlantic City. The day he arrived, a contractor was hired to paint the gym. He also was the biggest heroin dealer in Atlantic City, and residents of IHD flocked to buy his dope. Billy's roommate had a set of works, which Billy borrowed, and he began shooting up. There were male and female residents in the program, and they were going to bed with one another. People were climbing in and out of windows making brief escapes. To Billy this program was nothing but a joke, reinforcing the hopelessness of his situation to him. The world could offer him no help, no hope.

After two weeks, Billy walked away. He went to West Orange and stayed at his mom's apartment. Alone and on his own because Helen was working in New York, Billy went right back into drugs and stealing. He met a person influential in the Mafia who would buy his stolen goods. Billy was not feeling good about having left the program, so he asked Marty, his Mafia friend, if he could help. Marty had friends in the legal system, and he talked to the chief probation officer. No problem, Billy was assured, so he turned himself in. But where was the officer when Billy went before the judge? He never showed up, and Billy was re-sentenced to four years at Leesburg. This wasn't what he expected! Feeling this was unfair, he put in a petition and was able at least to have his sentence reduced by the amount of time already served.

In Leesburg Billy was incarcerated with an infamous prisoner. Tommy had killed two police officers after torturing them in the Angel's Inn bar. Newspaper headlines read, "The Night the Devil Came to Angel's Inn." Tommy and his partner became hunted men. When Tommy heard that his buddy had been gunned down, he knew that they wouldn't play around with him. He went to a priest; the priest called the news media, and Tommy was arrested. He had been in prison 22 years when Billy arrived. He and Billy worked the same detail and ate at the same cafeteria. In prison he was viewed as a hero. After all, he had killed two of the enemy. Billy thought Tommy was kind rather than a criminal. Crimes are viewed in a different perspective behind bars. Prisoners have a code of ethics all their own. Only a few things are not heroic, including rape and child molesting. A child molester might have to spend his days in solitary confinement for his own protection.

Billy's wit and sense of humor helped him out in prison. The prison maintained a large farm, supporting itself with milk, fruit and vegetables, etc. Shortly after his return, Billy saw his name on a list for transfer to the farm. He was puzzled by the assignment, for he was in medium security and the farm was minimum security. He was not ready for this kind of freedom and the trouble he knew it would bring. It would be far too easy to just walk away. It was near Christmas. Billy thought how nice it would be to be home. He began singing, "I'll be home for Christmas...", and "Over the wall, and through the woods..."

Billy went to the main center keeper in administration and told him of the mistake. "You send me to the farm, and I will escape." The prison officials already recognized his charismatic personality. One guard in particular sensed that Billy could be trouble, and he did not want to be bothered with such a pest. He told Billy, "Look, you don't make my job hard, I won't make your time hard. The only one who can take your name off that list is Miss Shirley McPherson, the prison psychologist."

Billy had a brief conversation with himself. "Self," he said, "you can't get far in prison attire. Escape is not a good option." But knowing himself, he knew going to the farm put him in danger of doing just that, if for no other reason than for the challenge it offered. So, after this interview with himself, he sought an interview with Miss McPherson. A guard gave him a pass to her inner sanctum. When she asked what the emergency was, he replied, "I know of a prison break."

"Tell me about it," she said.

"It's the list for the farm. If I go, I will escape, and I don't want to," was his reply. Miss McPherson read him like a book.

"Where are you from?" she asked.

"New York," Billy replied.

"People from New York never want to go to the farm. Just what do you do here?" she asked.

"Oh, I play chess. I read. I write poetry."

"Poetry? How good are you at poetry?"

"Pretty good," replied the confident, charismatic Billy.

"Good enough to write a poem about why you shouldn't go to the farm?"

"Well, I can try," returned the prisoner, and off he went. Soon a jingle began to rhyme in his head, and he returned to Miss McPherson with this poem:

The Farmer in the Cell

The food we eat ain't finger-licken'
Don't know a thing about a chicken,
Don't know about a twig or log,
Or the difference between a pig or hog.

Now I don't want this to sound alarming,
But I didn't come here to do no farming,
I didn't come to disobey,
Or pick no cotton, or roll in hay.

Ain't shovelin' no pit,
Don't want no part of it,
Ain't feedin' no cow,
'Cause I don't know how.

Now send me to school to take a few courses,
So I can to learn to be one of the bosses,
'Cause as I sit and write my rhyme,
I mind my business and I do my time.

So with that I bid farewell,
From the farmer in his cell.

Miss McPherson thought it was good, so good that she gave it to Mr. Beliki, head of the farm. Billy was let off farm duty, did his time, and caused no trouble. Later Mr. Beliki was transferred to medium security. Billy met him in the hall one day and said to him, "Mr. Beliki, you know me, but you don't know me."

"How can that be?"

"Well," said Billy, "I'm the farmer in the cell."

"Oh!" Mr. Beliki grinned. "That was so good, I had it blown up and it's been hanging on my office wall ever since!"

Billy wrote several other poems during this prison stint, including "Madness," "Poison," and "The Auction." These poems are now registered in the Library of Congress.

Billy was paroled from Leesburg on December 22, 1985. He had gone before the parole board a year earlier, but parole was denied. Christopher Dietz, head of the parole board in New Jersey, had presided at his hearing. The word in prison was that Mr. Dietz was famous for denying parole. Sure enough, he denied Billy, but said to him, "Keep your nose clean, and you'll be home by next Christmas." Now, a year later, Billy again went before the board. It was December 15, and Mr. Dietz was again presiding.

Billy was ready for him. He had found a piece of two-inch-wide ribbon and made himself a tie, which he wore along with his prison clothing. Nobody wore a tie before the parole board – except Billy Schneider, that is.

When Billy's turn came, he answered a few routine, goal-oriented questions: "If released, where would you go? What would you do?" Parole was approved. "Mr. Schneider, we will release you on February 2, 1986." Billy should be happy, right? Wrong. He just had to speak up for himself, so he stood up, thanked the parole board for the approval, then turned to Mr. Dietz. "Mr. Dietz," he said, "I know that you are a man of integrity. I was hoping you'd stick to your word."

"And what was that, Mr. Schneider?"

"When I came before the board last year, you said I'd be home by Christmas."

"I don't recall saying that!" Mr. Dietz replied.

"You do have the records, don't you?" (Parole board interviews are recorded, word for word, as are any court hearings.)

"Mr. Schneider, I gave you a February release date. However, on my lunch hour I'll go over these records. If I said it, I'll change. As a matter of fact, let's check the records right now." He did, and found that Billy had remembered correctly.

"Well, Merry Christmas, Mr. Schneider. And by the way," he added, motioning Billy close to him, "nice tie. It was one of the reasons I paroled you. But don't tell anybody. I don't want everyone coming in here wearing one!"

So, Billy was leaving in a week. He called his mom. "Hi, Mom. I'll be home for Christmas!"

Billy took the bus from Leesburg to Newark and picked up from his parole officer his release money earned for work in prison ($1.50 per day). He then went home to his mom's apartment in New York City.

Two months later, on February 6, 1986, his Uncle Sonny died.

William Schneider looks bewildered as he is taken to a police car.

Photo by Josh Barbanel

Man Climbs Bridge
In Plea for Help

By JOSH BARBANEL

William Schneider of W. 187 St. was desperate. By his own account he was heavily involved with drugs and a patient at a methadone maintenance clinic. He had a long police record for minor burglaries and car theft. He wanted help.

To dramatize his plea, last Friday morning he walked across the pedestrian walkway of the George Washington Bridge and began to climb the wide steel beams of the 400 foot support tower on the Manhattan side of the bridge.

Schneider, 27, scurried up the steel beams until he was fifty feet from the top of the bridge, 550 feet above the Hudson River, and threatened to throw himself off if he couldn't get help.

After snarling traffic on the bridge for two hours, a priest and (continued on page 9)

Billy –1950

Billy & Danny with Aunt Dorothy –1952

Billy, Age 6 –1955

Billy, Age 8–1957

*Billy, with Neighbor &
Mother out of window–1957*

*Schneider Boys –1955
Billy, Bobby, Danny*

*Schneider Boys with Mom–1960
Danny, Billy, Bobby*

Sonny with sons
Danny & Billy–1961

Schneider Family at Bobby's Wedding –1966
Danny, Bobby, Susan (Bobby's wife), Billy's Mom
Helen, his Dad Sonny, Billy (age 17)

Linda, Bobby, Billy
June–1970

Billy's 21st Birthday
with Linda–1970

Billy–1970

Linda, Age 19 –1972

Billy with Billy Jr. –1974

Billy & Linda Newlywed –1972

Billy & Linda with Billy Jr. –1974

Billy with Billy Jr. –1975

Billy, just out of Prison
Christmas –1985

Billys' 1st day at TLC –1987

Billy & his Mother Helen
Easter–1987

Billy Jr.–1991

Billy & Linda –1991

Billy & Sarah McCorkle–1994

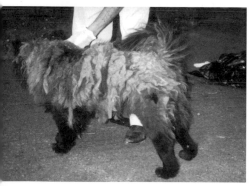

Edderic Patheteric, Just Found–1996

Billy with Linda's Parents
John & Evelyn, September–1996

Billy, Midnight, & Joanne May –1997

*Billy doing what he does best,
witnessing on the streets of NYC.*

*GOTeL Ministries
Billy & Paul T. Fleming*

*Billy speaking at a
School Assembly*

Ode to Billy Schneider

I once was privileged to have met,
A very special man, I'll never forget.

The constant smile on his face,
My mind can never simply erase.

Some smile for love of money,
Some smile for their "honey",

But the smile on his face,
Is the glow of God's great grace.

He's gone through more than you could ever know,
But time after time, Jesus' love he does show.

He doesn't tell you he's dying,
He doesn't walk around crying,

He doesn't say woe is me,
He doesn't beg, steal or plea.

Praise God he decided not to jump,
Praise God his old ways he chose to dump.

His life has been filled with misery & trial,
Just ask the "Judge" to look through his file.

Your everyday man would give up and get bitter,
But Billy Schneider is not a quitter.

His earnest desire is not to gain fame,
But just to bring praise to God's precious name.

He's a witness that life truly is not a game,
So he surrendered that life for Jesus to claim.

Today Billy has only one care,
Will he see you up there?

by Stephanie Brown
1994

Billy "Schneitz" Schneider

He came into our lives, one Sunday in November
His smile and loving nature, will stay with us forever
He shares the gift of Christ's salvation
To those in need across our nation
This man named Billy was called to tell
How drugs and sin will lead to hell
Oh, don't be afraid, it doesn't end there
Jesus died and named us his heirs
His love will take you to greater heights
Just listen to my good friend Schneitz

by Annette Kok
1995

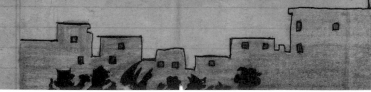

To My Son
    With All My Heart and Soul
Hoping This Little Letter Finds You In Good
Health and   Spirits

Your Father Really   I Hope you really
Feels Ashamed   Like it There
But He Is Not The   Mommy and Daddy
One To Blame   Do Care.

I Really Love You   But Certain Things
    Billy Boy   Just Happen Son
You"Ll Always Fill   Not Just to you
My Heart With Joy   But Everyone.

I Never Want To   Someday You'll Grow
Hurt You Son   To Be a Man
Or Ever Hurt   So Start Today
    Anyone   And make A Plan

I wish I could   Don't Do The Things
  explain   Some People Do
What Fills My Heart   That Makes Them Sad
With all This Pain   And Always Blue

But Always Try
To Do Your Best
And Fill Your
Life With Happiness.

I Wish That I
Could Try To Hide
These Tears That
Fall From My Eyes

This World Today
Is Full Of Hell
And Let That Word
Ring A Bell

Dont Make Your Hell
Like Daddy Did
Or You Will Have
To Write Your Kid
And Tell Him All
The Things You Did.

But Find A Star
Tonight And Pray
Tomorrow Will Be
A Brighter Day.

8-14-83

I'make Another
Promise Kid.
Not To Do The
Things I Did

And Then The Day
Will Come My Son
We'll Reach Our Star
And Have Our Fun

I Love You Son
And Always Will
And This Is Something
No One Can Kill.

I'm Sorry From
My Heart And Soul
But Certain Things
I Cant Control

I'll End For Now
My Little Letter
Hoping Things Will
Get Much Better

With All My Love And
For Your Joy, I'm So
Proud Your My Boy.
Love Always Daddy.

By a hurting Dad, while Billy was in
Leesburg State Prison & Little Billy
was at "Children's Village" (age 9),
a home for troubled children

poison

There are many many poisons
for rats mice and men
but drugs to me have got to be
the strongest poison.

They say the King is heroin
but many can take his crown
for I'll just list a few
that can take a good man down.

I listened last week, to five men speak
of how they took their fall
they all spoke of their horrors
from a drug called alcohol.

Still on the list of majesty
and next to take his place
a close and second runner up
in this Oh royal race.

Some die, some kill, and many slain
and wind up in a ditch
some call her girl, but boy, is she
a nasty little witch.

She had me climb a bridge one day
I didn't want to die
the doctor's called me crazy
I often wonder why?

But I'm not the one who's crazy
nor am I insane
all rise to greet her majesty
the deadly Queen cocaine.

There's L.S.D. and T.H.C.
and pills that come assorted
some injected, some you eat
some are often snorted

But no matter how they're taken
the life you live you're faking
you'll never, ever be yourself
your destiny is plain, for I am now
residing at satans house of pain.

It's a pain that I call loneliness
its felt from deep within
I only need my faith right now
and no more poison..

By William Schneider
A.K.A. Billy Words 6/83/90 A.D.

Written in 1983,
Caligraphied in 1990

CHAPTER 12

Nearing the End of the Line

Billy went to work for Gem Carpet Company. An opportunity came up to tile kitchens and bathrooms in a large apartment complex, and Billy found himself in charge of tiling 285 units. He got his Uncle Charley and his cousin, Joe Parker, jobs helping him. None of them was experienced at this kind of work, but with a little of Billy-style ingenuity, they got the job done. After this large job, business was slow, and Billy spent time at a bar across the street from his mom's apartment. Next to the bar was a pizza parlor owned by Marcos. Marcos used to hang out in the bar. He got a kick out of Billy, especially when he pretended to play a saxophone. He thought Billy was funny without trying to be. And he was right. Billy was naturally hilarious.

Billy began hanging out with Marcos at the pizza place. One day Billy helped Marcos out at the counter, handing out slices and serving sodas. Marcos tossed him a $20 bill, and Billy went home.

The next day, he was back with Marcos. Several times throughout the day, Marcos said that he would like to get out of the business. "I'd just like to walk away!"

About 3 p.m., Billy said to him, "Here, let me make a pizza."

"You can't," Marcos replied.

"Try me. I can!" So Billy put on an apron, threw together some dough, tossed the dough in the air, and voila! He was a natural-born pizza man. About 5 p.m. Marcos went to the register, pulled out some money, took off his apron, turned around and said to Billy, "I'm going to give you the break of your life. You can have everything in this store – machines, food, the money in the till. I've just got to talk to Sammy."

He came back 20 minutes later with Sammy, who said, "You understand, this is half my business. I require so much rent per week. But I've got a way to help you out." Marcos and Sammy were selling cocaine.

"We'll tell you who our customers are." And with two hours' experience, Billy found himself proprietor of a pizza parlor.

Marcos stayed on for the next two days, not to teach Billy the ropes of pizza making or restauranteering, but so that Billy could learn who all his cocaine customers were. Doctors, nurses, prostitutes and hustlers – all filtered through this shop looking for their fixes. Selling pizza was just a front. But not for Billy. He enjoyed making pizza. He put in video games, a new rage for the age, played "oldies" on the radio and hung a big sign, "No Swearing!" With every large pizza order, a customer could pop a balloon and pay the price marked in the balloon. Billy put up twenty-five balloons per day with six containing coupons for free pizzas. The balloons went daily. His family-oriented business did well.

Billy staged video tournaments. Five dollars would cover the cost of entering, a slice of pizza and a soda. Billy's prizes were $50, $35, and $25, not bad earnings for a kid. And Billy made money himself.

Billy's side business also boomed. Billy pocketed $35 for every $100 worth of cocaine he sold. Coke customers would come in just like any other customer and buy pizza, and Billy would also fill their side orders. Some would come in and ask Billy, "Where's Marcos?" and Billy would know to page Marcos, for these were his larger customers. Marcos had his cocaine coming in directly from Florida. The largest amount Billy would sell was one gram, at $100 per gram. This could be stepped on (cut) six times and still be salable. Cocaine could be cut with a number of things – vitamins, Inositol, speed.

It is remarkable that when a person buys a drug on the street, he trusts the most untrustworthy people in the world with his very life. He has little or no idea what is in the drug he is buying. Billy knew a man on the streets of New York City who used to be called "the Claw." In the 1970s, heroin would sometimes be cut with meat tenderizer. If a vein was missed, this mixture would start an abscess in the tissue. The Claw was a meat tenderizer victim. His arm weighed about 40 pounds and was filled with abscesses. He kept it wrapped in a plastic bag, and whenever he was out and about he would carry that arm, cradling it with his left arm. Billy wondered why his shoulder was always covered with flies. One time Billy saw the Claw's arm, and it was the most gross, putrid thing he had ever seen. Not only was it abscessed and foul smelling, it was covered with maggots. The news on the street was that the Smithsonian Institution wanted to remove this arm and put it on display. They were willing to pay a large sum of money, but the Claw refused. About a month and a half later the Claw died, and on the street the word was the Smithsonian got the arm.

Within a short time, Billy was making more money on pizza than on cocaine. He still was living with his mom, who was unaware of the cocaine dealing. She used to come into the pizza parlor and help Billy just for something to do. Billy felt a bit guilty about this, realizing that if he were busted she would be an innocent victim. She was as deceived by the family-oriented atmosphere as anyone else.

With Billy doing so well selling pizza, why take the risk involved with selling cocaine? It wasn't the money. The main attraction for him was the women it brought in. Women were always attracted to Billy, and for him this was a bit of icing on his cake. Sometimes, in return for sex, Billy would give them a bit of extra cocaine.

It was not long before Billy began feeling the same frustration Marcos had felt. He was a pizza parlor prisoner, working six days a week, from 10 a.m. until 11 p.m.

In his small amount of spare time, Billy began to hang out with Jerry Hughes. Jerry was a doorman on Park Avenue. One day the two of them went to the "Regis and Kathy Lee" show. They had a good time together. Relaxing and having fun made both of them desire drugs. "Man, I feel like shooting up," Jerry said, echoing Billy's thoughts. In the four months since his release from prison, Billy had been drug free.

Billy decided to open late and went shopping. In the Bronx, he bought Jerry a bag of heroin. Jerry never could buy dope, because people always thought he looked like a plainclothes detective. Well, Billy thought, why not? He bought himself a bag as well. He got someone to work the pizza place and left by 4 p.m. to go to a party with Jerry. And the months of being clean went right down the drain.

The place Billy bought heroin was called "Happy Face." Billy and Jerry had a little code, "You got a happy face today," meaning one of them wanted heroin. Then Jerry would watch the store and pay cab fare for Billy to go for dope. To Jerry it was an occasional thing, but for Billy, heroin was a monster. Jerry did not understand this.

Billy started out snorting, but very soon he got a set of works and started shooting not only heroin, but cocaine as well. Because cocaine was so readily available to him and because it was sexually arousing, he used it more than heroin. Billy returned to pornography, and his downward spiral began once again.

Billy was attracted to a girlfriend of a friend. One night after closing the pizza store, he met up with Laurence. She wanted cocaine, but did not have enough money. Billy took some from the store, and with no better place to go, went with her to the rooftop of a nearby building. They went through a lot of coke, but who cared? They were having fun. Finally near morning, Billy said, "One more hit, and we'll make it good." Billy mixed a syringe full and Laurence shot up. She was greedy and took the whole shot at once. As Billy started to shoot up, Laurence began convulsing. Billy panicked. "Laurence!" he screamed, trying to rouse her. He tried to feel her pulse, but could not. He tried mouth-to-mouth resuscitation and punched her in the stomach and the chest, but to no avail. He was convinced that she was dead.

Suddenly, she regained consciousness but was hysterical. She ran crazily up half a flight of stairs to the next roof level then down the fire escape. Billy did not try to follow her. Soon he heard glass breaking . . . then silence. Billy was terrified. He was convinced that she lay dead in the alley below. He went home to his mom's apartment, nervously expecting to hear the wail of sirens, but he heard nothing. He was too terrified to go out and look for her. And for sure, he could not sleep.

At 9 a.m. he opened the store. From there he was able to see across the street. He alternately paced the floor and stared out the window. He thought that Laurence had stolen a gram of coke from him because it was missing from his stash. Had she taken that as well during the night, causing her to OD? His mind just would not stop racing. "She's dead. I'm responsible. And worse, I'm doing nothing to help!"

With these thoughts terrorizing him, he continued to gaze out the window. Suddenly he blinked as he saw Laurence come out of the building, stopping to pick something up off the ground. Billy was relieved to see her alive and angry at her at the same time. Yes, she had taken the coke. That was what she picked up from the ground as she sauntered toward the pizza parlor.

It was the most frightening event of Billy's life. He never had seen a cocaine overdose, and he had not known what to do. For hours he had imagined her in her frantic state falling from the fire escape. In reality, the glass he had heard breaking was a window panel sitting on the fire escape that in her haste she had knocked down. She had jumped into her own apartment through a window and gone to bed, unaware of the panic she caused Billy.

Billy was sick of the pizza business, but even more sick of the cocaine. He was angry at Sammy for putting him, a known addict, into this terrible position. Billy felt that if he left on good terms he likely would be back for cocaine. He decided the only way to go was to burn this bridge, so one morning he began giving away everything in the store. Next door Sammy watched incredulously as customers went away with his cash register, soda machine, food, pizza — everything. Sammy was helpless, for he certainly couldn't call the police! And he was sure he couldn't outwit Billy. So when Billy walked in and handed Sammy the keys, he just took them. Billy's dream was over. What a crazy deal this had been! But the neighbors were sorry to see him go. His pizza had been good, his place fun and seemingly clean.

During this time Billy had seen Linda a time or two. Soon she sent little Billy to see his Dad and ask for money for a pregnancy test. Billy thought she just wanted drug money and ignored the request. But Linda was pregnant, and she soon had an abortion. It was a terrible position for an 11-year-old to serve as the go-between in a situation too complicated even for adults.

Billy's mom, horrified by the rapid downward spiral she saw in her son, called his parole officer. Billy called him a few days later, and, because he was habitually late, his officer asked him to come in. As soon as he was seated, his parole officer said, "Wait here just a minute." When he returned, it was with two police officers. "You're under arrest for violation of parole." Billy was handcuffed and returned to prison to complete his sentence.

The next night, in the apartment three doors from his mom's, two people were murdered. On Saturday morning, Billy called his mom from prison. She made a habit of never accepting collect calls, but this morning she did. "Your life may have been saved by being arrested," she told him. The apartment where the two people had been murdered was where Billy hung out and purchased drugs, and had he not returned to prison he likely would have been there.

Billy was released on October 22, 1986, but to what? He had not been rehabilitated from drugs. He was alone and homeless. At times on the street, both cold and hungry, he would think, "In prison they're lining up for dinner now." What was there in life for him "on the outside?" He was tired. Tired of life.

CHAPTER 13

From Death to Life

One by one, family members, friends, and acquaintances were dying. Their lifestyle began to take a grim toll of death.

First there was Scottie, who in 1965 sniffed glue, became dizzy, and fell over a cliff into the street below. He was buried by his grieving Jewish family within twenty- four hours.

Then there was Chata, Billy's first Dominican friend, who could not speak a word of English when he started school, murdered by his own best friend.

And Richie, whose mother, in one weekend, was called by the police twice. First, Richie had been beat up. The second time he had OD'd, and was dead.

His friend Bobby Dillon died of an overdose.

Tony Janero, dead. Tony's father was a prize fighter. He once fought Jake LaMotta, and the movie "Raging Bull" includes footage of this fight. Death did not bypass the rich or the famous, and Billy's friend Tony was found dead in Greenwich Village of a drug overdose.

"T-Bird," dead of hepatitis. People on the streets bragged about how many times they had "hep." Suddenly, it wasn't quite so cool.

Billy had witnessed the death of a fellow drug user in front of the Methadone program.

His father was dead.

Butchie Link, dead of a suicidal overdose. Butch left a note that said, "Nobody loves me, nobody cares." Billy wanted to shake him and cry to him, "Why didn't you call me?" Butchie's mom, out of her mind with grief, cried to Billy, "Please! Wake him up! Look! He's all dressed, ready to go to work!" as if Billy could bring him back from the casket in which he lay.

Uncle Sonny, Billy's hero, dead and gone.

Bob Riley jumped off the George Washington Bridge.

TK, Ritchie Robles, Marty Feldman, Eddie Hand, all dead. The party was winding down. It was no longer fun.

Billy was at the end of his rope. It was late 1986. Recently released from prison, he was once again using heroin and cocaine. Instead of being home for Christmas, he spent the holidays at Rikers Island, sentenced to ten days for trying to steal a hot dog stand. And where, oh where, was home? After his release, he spent two weeks on the streets of New York City, totally alone. For five days straight he did not eat or sleep. Someone alerted his mom, and for the first time in her life, she walked the streets looking for him. On hearing this, Billy thought maybe he could get some money from her for more drugs, so he found his way to her apartment. He sat down in her recliner and passed out from fatigue and hunger. Helen immediately called an ambulance, and Billy was taken to Columbia Presbyterian Hospital.

For three days Billy lay in the hospital, his legs swollen from malnutrition and frostbite. He was treated for a venereal disease as well. Drugs had taken a tremendous toll on his body. He might be the next to die. He reviewed his life. In 1967 he had been sentenced to prison for the first time. In the years since, the numerous times in prison never changed him or helped him. In 1977 he climbed to the top of the George Washington Bridge to plead for help. The world to which he cried out did nothing for him. No matter what he did, nothing changed. Nothing the world offered was fun any more. Friends were dying; relationships meaningless. Now, in 1987, his heart, his mind, and his body were sick and near death.

Billy's condition was desperate, but he was not quite ready to give up. He had been in the hospital three days and was improving slightly when he spied a camera left behind by a nurse. Camera in hand, Billy sneaked out of the hospital, sold the camera, bought cocaine, met a girl walking the streets, invited her to visit and share his cocaine, and returned to his hospital bed to get high. He hid his street clothes in the bathroom ceiling, planning an escape for the next day as well. The girl visited and stayed most of the night. No one in the hospital seemed to notice any of this.

The next day, with still a bit of money from the camera, he got his clothes from the ceiling and repeated his escapade. Returning again with cocaine, he found a gospel tract lying on his bed. He had no idea who left it there. Seeing the tract, he realized, "That's it. God is talking to me. I don't have much time to listen. Actually, I'm already dead, I just need a burial." Billy read the tract, a testimony by his old friend Tom Mahairas, with the Manhattan Bible Church address stamped on the back. With nothing to lose, he called Tom. Tom came to see him, telling

Billy he had choices, but they were his to make. Tom, two doctors and Billy talked the situation over. The doctors were making the usual plans for discharge – welfare, medical assistance, Methadone. Tom offered him Jesus, and the Transformation Life Center. TLC is a one-year, Christ-centered, drug-rehab program, operated as a ministry of the Manhattan Bible Church, located in the mountains of upstate New York. The choice was Billy's. He considered, but made no decision. Instead, he returned to the streets, back on heroin. Within a matter of days he needed detox, so he signed himself into St. Luke's detox center. After a week, Billy called Tom: "I'm ready to go to TLC."

Tom wanted to make sure he was serious, so he asked him to come around to the church, do odd jobs, be in the services for two weeks, and stay off drugs during this time.

Billy came into the church during a basketball game, his blue jeans stained with blood from injecting drugs, his body frail. Tom came over and put his arm around him, introducing him as his best friend. Over the next two weeks Billy sporadically came to church, not keeping up his end of the deal, continuing to do drugs, and hanging out with friends wherever he could find them.

On Friday, February 13, Billy came to a men's prayer fellowship at the church. He prayed, "Lord, please open the doors for me to go to TLC." Tom felt his prayer was sincere, and the next morning he headed for TLC with Billy and Oscar Aquino, another man in need of drug rehab.

It was in the van that Billy met Jesus face to face. As he sat, miserable from drug withdrawal, he knew the fight was over. The games were ended, the world had beaten Billy. He was finished. "Lord, I'm yours. You can do what you want with me, but I'm through. The streets beat me. You fix me. I need a fix for my heart. The real fix. Lord, please let this be real!" He thought of what had, or hadn't happened, when he had raised his hand in church in 1978 and nothing had changed. He could not face that again. Either Jesus was the real thing or he was not. And now that everything else had failed, Billy was ready to give him a try.

As he prayed, he began to hear an answer. "Jump!" Billy had heard that word before. It instilled fear in his heart. He had heard it as a tiny boy, and it caused him pain and panic. He had heard it from the top of the George Washington Bridge, the crowd below daring him. He had heard it echoing back from the despair of his own heart, "Why not jump?" He had heard the mockery in his father's drunken words – "Go ahead and jump!"

Now he heard it again. This time there was no dare, no mocking, no insult. Only a whisper, "Come to me..." Billy saw the arms of Jesus, stretched out to catch him. "Go ahead, Billy. Jump!" He saw the tenderness, the compassion in the eyes, and heard it in the voice that reached across the years, from the cross to his heart. "Come on, Billy! I'll catch you!" At last Billy gave up, and jumped into the arms of Jesus. This time, there was blood, but it wasn't Billy's. There was pain, but Billy didn't feel it. It was Jesus' hands that bled, it was Jesus' body that was wounded. And it was Billy who was healed. And Jesus said, "Happy Valentine's Day, Billy! Today I'm your Valentine!"

As they neared TLC, Billy was desperate for a cigarette. He had no idea what to expect, but he was in for a culture shock. It was a wintry day, and he was not much impressed with the creek (the summertime swimming hole) that Tom pointed out to him, shrouded in ice and looking a lot like he felt.

Arriving at TLC, Billy saw a few unimpressive metal buildings nestled in a basin in the mountains. The "life center" looked like a ghost town. Finally there were signs of life as people came to unload the van, and Billy could see the excitement on their faces because Tom had come. Billy was miserable, sharing none of their enthusiasm. Inside he sought a bit of warmth from the pot-bellied stove in the kitchen area. It was not much help. Around him, everyone was dressed up for the Valentine's Day banquet, with wives visiting for the event.

After a couple of hours, Billy was exhausted. He couldn't keep his eyes open. His body was weak. He would doze off for a few seconds, feeling like it was hours, drooling as he progressed into withdrawal. Finally someone saw Billy drooling and dozing and suggested he be brought upstairs and given a bed. Billy thought that Bill Rozenberger, who showed him the way, looked like Charles Manson. In his confusion, Billy thought to himself, If this guy offers me Kool-Aid, I'll knock him out! It was a rather unconventional beginning for Billy's new life in Christ.

Bob Ivins, the director of TLC, was as concerned for Billy's physical life as he was for his spiritual life. This guy's a goner, Bob thought. He looked so dark and fragile. His spirit was thin. How might he be helped? What could be done for him? Billy looked so bad that Bob was not sure he would live.

Billy awoke to a regimented, regulated environment – up at 6:30 a.m., your feet on the cold floor, brush your teeth, and be ready for "devotions," whatever they were. It was the newest word in Billy's vocabulary, he had no idea what it meant, or who to devote to. He had been found, but he still felt lost.

Billy was about to begin the hardest year of his life. He would come both to love and hate TLC. Learning to live with others would not be easy. In prison, there was no choice; you were there to stay. At TLC you could walk away any time you pleased. To choose to do something that was uncomfortable, that made him so miserable, was something Billy never had done before. He would have to make a daily choice to stay. He would find his choices narrowing, because to do wrong now would become oddly uncomfortable.

During withdrawal, Billy began to crave sweets. He knew where the cookies were kept. He sneaked into the kitchen in an army crawl, got to the cabinet, opened it from the bottom, and grabbed a handful of Oreos. He quickly made his exit but was filled with the strangest sensation – guilt! Tom had told Billy that Jesus would cure, heal, provide, and do a lot of other things. But he didn't tell him how all this would happen. And he didn't say a thing about Jesus convicting.

As "fate" would have it, Billy slipped and fell while making a dash for the next building, and the cookies crumbled. Billy put the "waste not, want not" law into effect and ate the cookies anyway. But in that moment, God showed Billy some things. First, that he indeed was a new creature, like it or not. The theft may have been only Oreos; however, God showed Billy in black and white what conviction meant. Billy knew he was in trouble with the Spirit of God. This man, who was a thief at heart, whom Uncle Sonny had taught well, now couldn't even steal a cookie. Billy also knew, in the aftermath of that incident, that he would be at TLC the whole year, no matter what. There would be no more running away from God. God had a firm hold on him. Now, Billy wondered how God would feel if he left. And how Tom would feel. Billy really was there for himself, but could he just walk away from a friend who truly wanted to help him? Billy knew he really did need Tom's help. He learned as well during that year that God was also his Friend, and that he needed His help. From now on, he knew he could never make it on his own.

Billy endured trial after trial, learning things he did not think he was capable of learning. The Bible began to be a recognizable friend. Later, when on the streets witnessing, he was surprised at what would pop into his mind. Things he had read in the Bible with his mind in a fog came back to him with clarity. For Billy, sharing his faith in Christ seemed natural. In the subway, the streets, and the parks, he began testing whether this new-found faith was worth sharing. He remembered that, as a drug addict, he was eager to share where the best dope, the best women, the best of the worst, could be found. Now, "addicted to Jesus," he became as eager to share the good news of salvation.

It was difficult learning to get along with the other residents. Now he could not walk away from them as he might have on the streets. Instead he had to learn to work out differences, solve problems, and love people who before would have naturally been his enemies. These lessons were extremely valuable.

Some of the men became friends whose relationships with him have brought incredible joy. Alan Rosenfeld was one. Adopted by Jewish parents, Alan's zeal for his Savior brought many around him to know Jesus Christ. Alan's zest for life was, if anything, even greater than Billy's. After graduation Alan first attended Word of Life Bible Institute, then Moody Bible Institute, and became engaged. Then, with the wedding planned, Alan began to feel stomach pains. At age twenty one, Alan died of cancer of the pancreas, a witness and testimony to all around him, even giving the gospel to the hospital chaplain who came to "cheer" him but who had no salvation message to offer.

Jerry Carella, whose family was a part of the Mafia, was another new friend. A man with a great sense of humor, Jerry later returned to TLC as the director.

There was Pete Carpio, known to all the residents as "Sweet Pete," a man whose demeanor never changed, and who later would seek Billy through tears when Billy took a fall.

And Jose Alvarez, who now has a lovely wife and daughter and a ministry to the homeless in Atlanta, Georgia.

Not everyone at TLC during that year succeeded. Oscar left the program and later died of AIDS. Doug returned to his old lifestyle shortly after graduation. Chuck, up and down afterwards, tested positive for HIV and returned to cocaine. Carlos went back on crack cocaine. Two others died of AIDS.

Everyone had to work in order to eat. Chopping wood, working on the buildings, and doing yard work were all a part of the program. Billy's job was in the laundry room. Even in this seemingly menial job he learned lessons. Now he tells new TLC residents, "When you come to TLC, bring all the dirty laundry of your life. Use TLC as a spiritual washing machine. You come in dirty, go out clean. Leave all your filth behind."

Not everything was hard work or demanding. Billy has wonderful memories of the camaraderie, fun and fellowship shared with both residents and workers. Bob and Robin Ivins were truly "parents" during this year. Learning to respect those in authority over him, Billy fondly remembers them as "Sister Robin" and "Brother Bob."

Billy finished the program at TLC in February 1988, although his graduation ceremony wasn't until May. The director decided to delay his graduation so he could graduate with a group. Nine men graduated that day. Billy left TLC and returned to New York, ready to start life as a new man.

CHAPTER 14

Baby Steps

As Billy approached his graduation from Transformation Life Center, he did not know what was next. He did not have a home to which he could return or family to support him, although his mom was happy and hopeful about the changes she saw taking place in her son's life. She attributed this change to Tom's influence, and possibly to "God" in his life. Billy's wife, Linda, was involved enough in his life to come to his graduation. But Billy no longer thought of her as a partner, nor did she wish to be a part of his life.

Billy heard from Tom that someone in the Manhattan Bible Church was interested in taking him into their home. One day he was talking to a friend, Charley Delph, and mentioned this to him. "What do you think I should do?" Billy asked him.

Charley replied, "If someone wants to help you, go for it!" Billy soon learned that it was Charley himself and his wife Shirley who wanted to take him into their home.

When Billy graduated, he accepted their offer. He came back to New York City and lived with Charley and Shirley. He started out doing odd jobs, taking "baby steps" back into the world, now as a new creature in Christ. This was a new chapter. Being "born again" is certainly the right choice of words for becoming a Christian. Jesus knew what He was talking about with Nicodemus. One starts out as a spiritual baby, with growth and development being gradual. TLC was the nursery for this newborn. Now he was graduated into elementary school. But for someone new in Christ, this is not always well understood. There is a tendency both for the new Christian and for those Christians around him who are older in the faith to forget the elementary process. Nursery, in whatever form it takes, is often deemed sufficient, and graduation is often straight from the nursery into adulthood. It is during this critical time that many new Christians fail. Often both they and those around them wonder why. Blame is placed and misplaced. Guilt ensues, and discouragement sets in.

That's why it was wonderful for Billy to be in the home of rock-solid believers who loved him, who encouraged him, and who continued to nurture him. It was good to be a part of the Manhattan Bible Church, a place where there were others who had gone through experiences similar to Billy's. The church accepted folks just where they were, but at the same time it stood for and taught the truth of God's Word. There was an elementary process going on, but the trials ahead for Billy were big ones. They would rock Billy, as well as everyone around him.

Within a few months after his graduation ceremony from TLC, along with friend Doug, he moved into the basement at the home of Henry Gross. Here he could be more independent, do his own thing, perhaps moving out of "elementary school." Along with Doug, he began his own business putting up vinyl siding. Things were going well.

Billy, however, knew he was at great risk for contracting HIV. The list of hazardous behavior was long – IV drug use, dirty needles, multiple sexual contacts, any one of which jeopardized his safety.

Satan began to plant seeds of doubt and fear in Billy's mind, whispering in his ear, "You coward! You wimp! You're afraid to be tested! What will your God do for you if you are positive? Huh? You think He's so good? How will He take care of you then?" Billy was taunted day after day by his enemy. AIDS was a very real threat. As time went by, Billy continued to walk with his God, but the enemy was wearing him down. At last he turned and faced his foe: "I am not chicken. My God will take care of me, and I'm going to prove it."

Billy was tested at the Bronx Lebanon Clinic. Then began a very long two-week wait. He could hear the seconds ticking away in his mind, "Tick, tick, tick...," the time slowly passing. The devil on his shoulder continued to taunt him, whispering "HIV, HIV, HIV or AIDS." It was never out of his mind. Words take on a strange twist. To be positive is negative. To be negative would be positive. To not know seems in some way better than knowing, as if a death sentence, delivered in those two terrible words – "HIV positive" – could be delayed by ignorance. With every passing second, Billy was reminded of his past. As moments ticked by he became more aware than ever that his past had not been a "high," it had been a "low." It had not been a dream, but a nightmare.

Now Billy learned what total dependence on God meant. What about God's promises on which he had been depending? If they were not true, what else in life mattered? Billy was certain that God was not a liar. He felt sure that God did not want him to be afraid. "The truth shall set you free," went through his mind. The "tick, tick, tick" quieted.

As he waited for the test results, he continued working. As he was putting vinyl siding on a home, Billy became friends with Bosco the dog. Bosco had no fear of Billy. He licked Billy's face, wagging his tail in greeting. Billy bonded with him, playing with him and even getting in Bosco's huge dog house with him. Seeing Bosco love him without reservation helped to soothe the inner fears Billy felt. It was as though God were speaking to him through the dog.

On July 27, 1988, Billy went back to the clinic to get the results, accompanied by Angelo Polihrom. Angelo was a deacon at the church who also was in business with Billy. Billy no longer was afraid. In his heart he knew what the results would be. Physically he was in good shape. In his spirit he had a peace promised by Christ, that all things would work together for good. He had no idea just how God would do this, but he was confident.

When the counselor told him he was indeed HIV positive, Billy responded with genuine happiness in a way that stunned the counselor. He had never seen a response like this. Billy felt such a sense of freedom from the grips of the Devil that he had a true joy in his spirit. He was free in a way the counselor could not understand. He could say with assurance that "Jesus' blood covers my blood!"

God already had spoken to Angelo's heart. When Billy came out of the counselor's office, his smile was so genuine that Angelo knew the results. He didn't say a word. He just gave Billy a huge hug. Billy thought this would be the reaction of all the church, his new family.

Billy called Pastor Tom and told him, knowing that Tom would know not to feel sorry for him. But Tom became very serious, so Billy said, "I'm sorry I messed up your day."

"Oh, no!" Tom responded, "It's just that I've known the Lord for twenty years. You've just met Him, and you're going to see Him before I do!"

Billy, lightening the moment, quipped, "Well, we could change that!" He did not look at this as an immediate death sentence. Who could know that?

Of course, Billy had no idea exactly when he acquired the virus. Was it important how long he had been HIV positive? At the time it certainly was, given the life expectancy for a person who was positive. But that was eight years ago, and Billy never has had an HIV-related illness.

As word of Billy's diagnosis spread through the church, Billy began to sense fear and withdrawal rather than the support and caring he needed. If he were standing near one door in the auditorium, he could see people begin to head out another door, avoiding coming near him. People were uncertain about what to say to Billy. Those who did speak to him would tap him on the shoulder by way of greeting rather than shaking hands or hugging him. Children always were attracted to Billy. Now Billy watched as parents would try to direct their children another way before they caught sight of him. Parents became very watchful, some literally running to catch their children before they were caught in an awkward moment and had to face their own fears.

On the one hand, Billy could understand the fear of his beloved friends. On the other, he was deeply hurt by those he thought he could depend on. Billy felt others build a wall around him, and he began to build his own emotional wall to shield himself from the pain of further rejection.

Billy had to learn to deal with HIV on his own. He was advised at the clinic to return for T-cell counts. In two weeks, he went back. His count was good. The doctor mentioned AZT, a drug used extensively in trying to hold off signs of AIDS in persons who are HIV positive. Although he was comfortable with the knowledge of the physicians at the clinic, Billy had no peace about taking this drug.

He continued to return to the clinic every two weeks to get his T-cells recounted. Most people he saw there appeared to be healthy. Their appearance, however, was deceiving, as every person there was HIV positive, and many of them had full-blown AIDS. People brought their children, and they played on the floor. What did this atmosphere do to them, their innocent eyes watching everything? Billy noted that it was not very clean. Blood was splattered on the floor in the area where patients sat to have their blood drawn. Could the virus be carried on shoes throughout the hospital, or out the doors on tiny fingers, playing on the floors?

The clinic became oppressive to Billy, and soon his main purpose in going there was to share Christ. He once had been eager to share needles, to share where to find drugs, and now he wanted to share Christ with the same energy. But he felt an overwhelming draining of his spirit. He felt pre-occupied with the virus, and subsequently with death. He would rather be concerned with life. He decided he would not continue to monitor his T-cells. Neither would he take medication. He felt that if he knew that his T-cell count were down, that knowledge itself could shorten his life. He did not want HIV to rule and direct his life. He determined to be Billy Schneider, child of God, who happened to be both HIV positive and JESUS-positive.

The wall that Billy built around his own heart remained. Billy was a people lover, and people loved Billy. His friends began to return to him, but Billy carried a reserve, a caution, developing a sense that he did not need others. Behind this wall he became lonely. In his solitude, he began to move away from God.

CHAPTER 15

Baby Falls Down

A week after Billy tested HIV positive, he made the difficult decision to tell his brothers. To tell his own family was harder than letting his church family know. He especially wanted to protect his mother. How could his brothers know without his mother finding out? Might the result of his sin prevent her from ever understanding a God who loved not only her son, but her as well?

He walked up Broadway toward Bennett Avenue, just blocks from where he had grown up. He met his brothers at their mother's apartment. He told his brothers that there was something he needed to say to them. Not wanting to tell them inside the house, he asked them to go out for a walk. Standing there on the street, huddled with his arms around them both, he spit out the words, "I have AIDS." Billy thought he could detect panic in the eyes of his brothers. And then Bobby responded. Tears came to his eyes; he grabbed Billy, gave him a hug and kissed him on the lips. "I love you!" he cried to Billy. What a reassurance from his brother! Billy asked his brothers to please protect Mom from the news. He wanted her to know only the love and joy of Jesus from him, not the awfulness of AIDS.

Billy felt an overwhelming sense of inner peace after he told his brothers. A weight was lifted from his shoulders. There would need to be no more denial; they had accepted him. To Billy it seemed much better if people knew. Then they could do with it what they pleased. Keeping the information secret was an unbearable burden, something Billy just did not want to have to deal with. Being open made him feel much better.

As they walked and talked, they neared their mom's apartment. She was looking out the window and saw her three sons all looking serious. Billy wondered if she somehow knew the truth. Being HIV positive made him feel almost as though his forehead were branded in scarlet letters – "HIV" – and that just to look at him was to know. Billy never told his mom about being HIV positive. But how can you shield a person as close as your mom from information that so many others have?

A friend innocently spoke to Helen of the HIV, and for years she lived in silent dread of Billy's death before she could share her knowledge and fears with her son.

A few days later, Billy again was at his mom's apartment building, sitting out front on top of a car talking to his brother Bobby. As they talked, he spotted a very attractive young lady coming down the street walking her two dogs. Gloria was a friend of Bobby's, but she was immediately attracted to Billy. Billy's eyes did it again!

Billy returned the next day, reasonably sure that he would see this young lady again. Sure enough, along came Gloria with the dogs. Being a dog lover gave Billy reason to walk around the corner with her. Within the next day or two he told her he was HIV positive. Gloria assured him that this did not matter to her. The attraction was mutual.

Gloria liked plants. Her office was being rearranged, and she was able to take home a very large plant if she could arrange for moving it. Billy got a hand cart from Henry Gross to help her out. In his pocket he put a $100 bill, thinking to take her to lunch. Somehow along the way the money was lost, and she ended up taking him to lunch on their first date. Billy felt her drawing close to him.

A web was being spun in which Billy was being trapped. Billy had left Transformation Life Center focused on the fact that drugs had been conquered. He did not recognize that there was more to conquer.

Billy began spending a lot of time with Gloria, going out for meals or to her apartment. There was a strong physical attraction developing, which was exciting to Billy. Depressed and feeling somewhat hopeless because of his HIV status, he had thought that an intimate relationship would never be possible for him again. Now it seemed within reach.

Did Gloria know the Lord? Would she be a spiritual help to Billy? On one occasion she came to the Manhattan Bible Church with Bobby, and both of them professed salvation. But that probably was as much as she knew about Jesus. The web was closing around Billy, and he did not realize it.

Gloria had been accustomed to using drugs. When she became involved with Billy, she stopped. However, one evening early in the relationship, Billy and Gloria were out with some of Gloria's friends, along with Billy's friend Doug. Gloria urged Billy to have a bottle of wine, but Billy hesitated. Even her friends discouraged her from pushing. Finally Billy decided, "What's a little glass of wine?" He had a drink. It was enough to mellow him and to encourage him to break through some of the boundaries he had learned to set as a born-again Christian. As he danced with Gloria, they both sensed a physical exhilaration, and that same night he went home and to bed with her.

Billy was entangled. Within a matter of weeks, this sexual relationship led him to move out of Henry Gross' basement into Gloria's apartment. Marriage was discussed, and the situation became an open affair.

Billy's brother Bobby was deeply hurt by this. He had thought of Gloria as his girlfriend and became jealous. Sometimes when he was drunk, he would stand outside her apartment window, calling Billy names.

If Billy and Gloria were to marry, there was a matter that needed to be settled first. Billy was still married to Linda. He and Gloria called Linda and made arrangements for the three of them to visit a divorce lawyer. Linda was agreeable, and they met at a lawyer's office right across the street from Billy's mom. The lawyer's secretary spoke with them, telling them what they would need to do. She would see that the necessary papers were filled out, and if Billy and Linda would return in about two weeks, she would have everything ready for them to sign. Billy paid the $200 fee.

Billy did not know it at the time, but Linda, who seemed so agreeable to the divorce, went from the lawyer's office across the street to her mother-in-law and wept in her arms. "I love him, Helen!" she cried.

It was September. Gloria began making wedding plans. A hall was secured for January. She began shopping and making a list of guests to be invited. Things were moving fast. It seemed as though everything was working together with amazing ease.

But once again, Billy's life was rollerblading downhill. With phenomenal speed, he went from a friendly encounter to a glass of wine to sexual relations to living together to moving toward divorce and remarriage. And it didn't end there.

Billy was becoming depressed. He began avoiding the Manhattan Bible Church. Out of God's will but not out of His reach, he was seized by an overwhelming sense of guilt, especially about the immoral relationship. He knew he didn't belong where he was.

Sometimes he would share this with Gloria. "God is not pleased."

She began to expect it, and would reply, "Don't start that! Don't beat yourself up! God understands our situation." And so Billy's conscience would be eased for a short time. It was not long before pornography began to creep into their relationship, a sure sign of dissatisfaction with each other.

Billy returned to Henry's place one day and found Doug shooting up. "What's the difference? A little wine, a little heroin?" Doug said. Billy, on his downhill journey, thought, What is the difference? A little heroin went into his system. "Hello, Billy. Welcome back." He could almost hear the drug talking to him. And he was back. Back in the pit of hell from which he had been rescued a year and a half earlier.

Billy brazenly walked into the church hand-in-hand with Gloria. Tom said, "Billy, you can't do this. You can't come to church hanging out with this woman. You don't know what you're doing." As a friend he pleaded with Billy, but Billy was not listening to any advice. "You can't run my life, Tom!" In his heart he knew Tom was right. And Tom didn't even know that Billy was once again addicted to cigarettes, cocaine, and heroin. He already was back to his old lifestyle.

The truth of the words of Ecclesiastes 7:26 was never more telling: "And I find more bitter than death the woman, whose heart is snares and nets, and her hands as bands: whoso pleaseth God shall escape from her; but the sinner shall be taken by her.(NIV)" Tom Mahairas used these words in pleading with Billy, but his heart was hardened. Billy was sure he knew what was best for himself. He had not yet tasted the bitterness, but it was coming. And Tom saw it.

Others pleaded with him as well: "Please, Billy, this is not the right thing! You've got to get out of this relationship." Billy basically told each of his friends to mind their own business. His heart was set on Gloria.

The church had to take care of its business too, and Billy was excommunicated. Tom's heart was broken, but Billy acted as though he didn't care. In spite of this attitude, Pete Carpio, one of Billy's friends from TLC, used to come by and throw pebbles at Billy's window to get his attention. He would cry, "I love you, Schneida!," ignoring the church requirement to have nothing to do with one who was excommunicated.

Meanwhile, things seemed to be going well for Billy and Gloria. One of Gloria's friends gave her a car, which Billy restored to mobility merely by installing a new battery. They put the car in her name, licensed and insured it. This gave Billy a way to get around, and he began driving Gloria to work, then heading out for a day of shoplifting, unbeknownst to her. Billy was deceiving Gloria as well as himself. At first she had no idea he had returned to drugs. But he could not keep this from her long. Jobs were scarce, but who needed to work anyway? This routine was familiar to Billy, and he began to fall into old habits.

Billy let five weeks elapse before getting back with Linda to sign the divorce papers at the lawyer's office. When they did return, there was had no more. The lawyer knew nothing about their papers, nor did he have their money. The secretary they had spoken to was no longer in the office. This woman had for some time been collecting money from and making promises to clients. She pocketed the money and had just recently disappeared. Their $200 had vanished with her, and there was no legal paperwork to show for it. But Billy had kept a receipt, and the lawyer gave him his money back. Much, however, had transpired in Billy's life during those weeks, and he now had second thoughts. He was no longer quite so taken with Gloria. Drugs once again were his lover, drugs met his needs, drugs quieted at least temporarily the terrible sense of guilt he was feeling, for God was not leaving him alone. He put off filing for divorce.

Deciding he needed Methadone, Billy called Linda. He gave her money and she would buy it for him. He knew that she would tap the bottle. Because of this he once stole about $30 from her to buy cocaine. Even though he thought she owed him, he felt guilty. The guilt just would not leave him alone. He was really getting low, because now when Gloria was at work, he carried on an immoral affair with Linda.

Gloria, however, wanted more security from Billy. Without Billy's divorce papers in hand, her wedding plans were shaky. Little Billy was not doing well in school, and Gloria felt that she could be a good influence on him. She thought she could help him more than his own mother could, and at the same time gain points with Billy. With a bit of pressure from her, young Billy came to live with Billy and Gloria. From the start little Billy disliked Gloria, and the atmosphere in the home was certainly no improvement for him. Billy began borrowing money from his enterprising son, who had a business selling candy and sometimes made as much as $200 a day.

When Gloria began bossing little Billy around, dictating how much time he could spend at Grandma's, Billy decided to move back home with his mom and Uncle Jimmy.

Gloria finally discovered that Billy was doing drugs and began to despise Doug for his influence on Billy. But Doug was not responsible for Billy's condition. Billy was responsible for himself.

One day Billy went into the Bronx and found Doug with his friend Tommy. Tommy had been saved, went to TLC, tested HIV positive, left TLC and went back on drugs. As Billy drove by, he saw the two of them getting beaten up by the police. They had stolen a car from someone Billy knew and then broke into a hardware store. With Doug and Tommy locked up, Billy went looking for the stolen car. After a short search, he found it unlocked. In the back seat hidden under a blanket Billy found about $3,000 worth of new tools. Billy transferred these to his (Gloria's) car, and for the next few days he was in the hardware business.

Doug got out of jail, and he and Billy hatched a great plan. Doug knew that a bag of heroin that went for $10 in New York was going for $25 in Pennsylvania. They decided to go to Doug's hometown in Pennsylvania where they would shoplift, return to New York, sell their goods, and buy heroin to resell in Pennsylvania. Billy did all the shoplifting, so he felt the money was all his. He brought back about $3,000 worth of watches and electronic goods to New York and sold them to his old connections for $900.

Billy and Doug made their way back to Pennsylvania in Gloria's car. On the way to sell the heroin, they stopped overnight in a motel. But they violated a cardinal rule of commerce as they began consuming their own goods. Billy taught Doug to mix heroin with cocaine. He woke up the next morning to find Doug shooting up in the bathroom. He had used a great deal of their heroin already. Angry, Billy began to detox Doug by shooting up in front of him and refusing to let him have any more drugs. He felt the drugs rightfully were his anyway because he had done all the work.

Now, in order to make money, they had to cut the drugs, and by the time they got to their destination, all they had left were worthless bags of garbage. They were in trouble. On top of that, they had car problems because they failed to add oil. Doug called a friend who picked them up and took them to Lancaster in exchange for two bags of heroin worth $50.

By now Gloria was both afraid and angry. She had the police put out a warrant for them for stealing her car. But what did they care? They were on foot, so how could anyone charge them for stealing a vehicle? Gloria and Billy talked on the phone from Doug's mom's house. Gloria wept, "We can work it out, Billy. Just come home!" Doug's mom wanted Billy away from Doug, so she gave Billy $40 for a bus ticket. Billy returned to New York City and spent the night in the Port Authority Bus

Terminal. Then he returned to Gloria's house, in his own words, "screwed up."

Two days later Billy purchased more heroin and entered an empty warehouse to shoot up. As he did so, he felt a horrifying sensation. Turning about, he saw a huge Satanic altar, and on it the remains of an offering – chicken parts, flowers, and other things. It was as though the icy hands of death were clutching at him. The himself he cried, as he had over and over, when shoplifting, when buying drugs, when shooting up, when involved in all kinds of sin, "What are you doing? You know the truth. What are you doing?" Tom's words came back to haunt him. They came straight from God's Word: "Turn him over to Satan, for the destruction of the flesh."

CHAPTER 16

Picked Up

In terror Billy fled the warehouse as if he were running from Satan himself. He saw the enemy for who he was, he saw the stain of his own sin. He had experienced enough. Now he was truly at the bottom. Before he had been at the bottom as a non-believer. Now as a sinner saved by grace, he saw that he had been spitting in God's face. He had been mocking God. And God now brought him to the brink of hell, allowing him to stare into the face of his enemy.

Billy returned to Gloria's apartment. Finding Gloria asleep, Billy quietly took the phone from her room. He feared what she might do if she heard him talking. She already was angry, knowing she might be losing him. Recently, when he spoke of his feelings of guilt, she had slapped him so hard on the ear that he temporarily lost his hearing. He did not want to risk awakening her now. He dialed Tom Mahairas's phone number from Gloria's bathroom. Tom's wife answered.

"Vicky!" Billy cried. "Please! I'm so hurting!" Tom was out of town. "Please, Vicky, pray with me!" Vicky did. Soon, Tom heard that Billy had called. He asked a couple elders of the church what he should do if Billy showed up at the next scheduled church event, the Friday evening men's Bible study.

Meanwhile, Billy talked to Pete Carpio. Were Pete's prayers being answered? He encouraged Billy to come to church.

Billy came to the Bible study. He fell to his knees and cried like a baby. It was decided then and there that Billy should go back to TLC. His willful spirit was indeed broken, and everyone there knew it.

The next day Pete took Billy to Gloria's to pick up his belongings. Gloria was furious. "You mean, just like that, you're leaving me? Is this what you call Christian?"

"Yes, Gloria, it is Christian. Living with you was not." None of Billy's actions with her had been Christ-like. Now he had to reap what he had sown by having been a poor example to her. No matter what he did now, it would hurt her. He could only extricate himself from his situation. He had been the greater sinner, since he knew the truth.

In January 1989, Billy returned to TLC for three long, hard months. Bob and Robin were no longer there. The atmosphere seemed military. But Billy was there for a purpose, and he stuck to it. He once again was captivated by God's amazing grace.

While he was there, Gloria filed legal papers making Billy responsible for many tickets on her car, which totaled more than $1,100. The price for sin was heavy, not only in lost time and lost testimony, but in money as well. In the following months Billy paid off the tickets on Gloria's car. He felt convicted to make restitution for his shoplifting, but he could not remember clearly enough what he had done or where he had been to make full restitution.

This time Billy began to learn about the weakness of the flesh. Salvation was much more than just becoming drug-free. There was a new life inside that was at warfare with the old life. The armor of God was meant for everyday use. Billy began to understand the meaning of Jesus' words, "Without me you can do nothing."

In April Billy once again left TLC, but this time with a much more humble spirit. He lived for a short time with Huey Wier. Huey bought Billy a pair of sneakers, a kindness Billy still remembers.

In May Billy was reinstated to membership at the Manhattan Bible Church. He is thankful that his church loved him enough to do the hard thing in disciplining him. He feels it was crucial in his return to the Lord.

CHAPTER 17

Coming Home

Even now, Billy sensed that something was not yet right in his life. Linda and little Billy began to come to mind on a regular basis. Surely God did not want him to return to Linda and a drug-filled, hopeless and depressing situation. But Billy heard God's voice. "What if it was Linda who had been saved? What would you think, how would you feel, if she did not come back to tell you about Jesus?" God asked. Put that way, Billy knew what he had to do.

He went to visit Linda in her dark apartment. Soon this became a daily habit. He would take Linda to the Methadone program or sometimes just sit with her. His prayers began to change, and his spirit softened. "Lord, if you want me to go back to her, teach me to love her. Let me see her like you see her." Linda was in poor physical condition, her beauty faded. She had lost all her teeth, and her youthful appearance was gone, dulled by years of self-abuse. The drugs made her like a zombie. She was empty, unable to carry on a conversation.

One day Billy asked her to go to church with him. To his surprise, she agreed. When he came to pick her up, she needed a pair of stockings, which he went to get for her. When he returned, he found her in tears. She had dropped her dentures in the sink, and a front tooth had broken and gone down the drain. "I can't go like this!" she wept.

Billy took the drain apart, but the tooth was not to be found. He felt bad for her, frustrated by what he saw happening. He asked her to give him her dentures. She did so, thinking he might try to fix them. Instead, he led her to a full-length mirror. "Open your mouth. You see, Linda, Satan already has robbed you of all your teeth. Don't let him keep you out of church because of one missing false tooth." Linda listened, and bravely went with him.

Soon after this, Billy made a decision to move back in with her. Linda was happy about it. Billy brought new life into her home. Linda's brother Jimmy had recently moved out, unable to handle the depressing atmosphere any longer. He had lived with Linda for fifteen years, and if anybody had been a father to young Billy, it was Jimmy. This move that seemed to make Linda's life even more hopeless was actually part of God's plan, paving the way for Billy's return.

Linda's life was lonely and dull. There was no fun in the drugs anymore. They were a trap that had sucked the life from her body as well as her mind. In Linda's spirit there now was a longing for something that was missing. She could sense this something in Billy as well as in his friends. She loved Alan Rosenfeld and his exuberance. From Alan she would listen to the gospel.

It was not an easy transition for Billy. Linda spent much time in bed or just sitting at home watching TV. Often her only outing was her trip to the Methadone clinic. Everything in the house looked and even smelled depressing. Billy began doing small repairs around the house. Noticing that the kitchen sink drained slowly, he took the drain apart. To his dismay, he found a hypodermic needle lodged in the drainpipe. Holding the needle in his hand, for the first time in many years he felt no lust for using one. Now it was more representative of the trash that had consumed so many of his years and had taken the lives of so many of his friends. At that point, he again questioned God: "God, are you sure you're not making a mistake?" He was certain he'd feel safer inside a lion's den, or perhaps hanging out with Shadrach, Meshack and Abednego. God reassured him, and Billy concentrated on fixing the drain, not on what had been clogging it.

He began to do other chores in the house, cleaning cabinets and washing counter tops and windows. The truth finally sank in for Linda as she saw him working. Coming through the door one day as she returned from her trip to the Methadone clinic, she made a statement that brought a smile to Billy's face: "Boy, you really are moving back in!"

Billy began to take charge of the home. He made certain that the rent was paid on time. He pleaded with the landlord to make major repairs in the apartment. Linda had lived there for nine years, and in that time no maintenance or repairs had been done. She was entitled to a paint job every three years, but she had not pursued even that.

Billy found that the landlord's agent had been letting late payments slide in exchange for sexual favors from Linda. At the same time, he let repairs slide, taking advantage of the fact that Linda was inebriated with drugs at all times.

Billy came home one day as the agent, George, was leaving. The next time he met George at the door and let him know that he knew what had been going on for the past seven or eight years. He also told him what he, as Linda's husband, would do about it.

Billy went after the landlord by way of the tenant's landlord court. In a matter-of-fact way, he explained to the judge what had been happening. Both judge and landlord respected what Billy said and the way he said it, and Billy won his case. The landlord allowed Billy to do the necessary repairs. He completely remodeled the bathroom and the kitchen. He took over for the painter the landlord had sent when he saw the poor job he was doing. When he was finished, he and Linda had the most beautiful apartment in the building.

Linda continued coming to church with Billy. One Sunday about a month after Billy had returned to Linda, Tom preached a sermon that Billy thought was not especially powerful. An invitation was given for salvation. Billy's head was bowed in prayer, but he could hear the sound of Linda's little feet shuffle past him. She made her way to the altar, and kneeling there, she asked Jesus into her heart. Billy was astounded. This was a decision made without prompting from him or from anyone but the Spirit of God. It was thrilling for him to see her kneeling at the altar in prayer! God was honoring Billy's faith in claiming the promise found in Acts 16:31 (NIV), "Believe in the Lord Jesus, and you will be saved – you and your household." The love God had put in his heart for Linda had melted hers. In him she truly had seen Jesus, and she was able to forgive the past.

Meanwhile, Billy had done one roof job which led to another, then another. Billy bought an old truck and was in business. God blessed this business, and his bank account began to grow. This was exciting for a man who had rarely kept a bank book in his life. Alan was helping Billy, but Billy really needed more help as he was getting so much business. He hired Linda's brother, Jimmy.

Jimmy didn't mind working for Billy, but Billy's religion irritated him. He felt rather religious himself; after all, he had gone to church and even taught Sunday school. He flatly stated, "I'm never going to that church with Billy."

However, one evening as they ate dinner together, Billy casually invited him anyway. "I'm going to church. You want to come along?" Because he had nothing better to do, he went with Billy to the midweek service.

When the congregation broke into small groups for prayer, Billy and Jimmy ended up in different groups. As they all came back together, Tom Mahairas said, "A man got saved here tonight. He had gone to church and even taught Sunday school. He thought he didn't need salvation. Jimmy, why don't you give a few words of testimony?" And Billy nearly fell off his chair as his brother-in-law got up, and in this church he vowed he would never attend, wept as he publicly stated that he had just accepted Christ! He said later that he had felt like garbage, lost, and empty. When he came into the church he realized just how alone he felt. Now he could join his sister in a new family relationship of being God's child along with her.

Linda's faith was simple. She began to read the Bible with Billy's help. But more often, she would listen to music tapes over and over. She enjoyed the "Footprints" poem, knowing that God must have been carrying her, as the poem describes.

On her own, Linda decided to withdraw from Methadone. She told the clinic what she wanted to do. She was on forty milligrams of Methadone per day and decided to drop by five milligrams every other week. This took about four months. Along with the Methadone, she had been taking twenty or twenty-five Benadryls per day. She needed to decrease and withdraw from them as well. The last five milligrams of Methadone were the hardest for her to let go. Not only was Linda addicted to the drug, but to the habit of taking it that had been with her for eighteen years. The faces at the program, the steps she took to the clinic, the train she caught a block and a half away, the cigarette she would pull out of her purse at precisely the same place in this daily trek, all were part of the habit. Billy was very supportive of her, happy that she had made the decision on her own, cheering every difficult step she took in removing the shackles of her addiction.

Withdrawal was hard on Linda. In the beginning, she would take her weekend doses on Friday. Once or twice Linda came home high on cocaine. Then, according to the terms of their agreement, Billy would not let her stay in the house. She had to find another place for the night. The second time, he put Oodie, her little cat, in her arms and said, "Here, take her with you." She protested, but he was adamant. If anyone knew the pain of addiction, of withdrawal, of deceit, of sliding backward, and of the need for tough love, it was Billy. These times were hard on them both, but Linda was tough. She never cried.

Linda had a strange habit, probably a rare "pica." A pica is a craving for an unusual substance, usually not a food item, which most often occurs during pregnancy. Ice, clay, and baking powder are some of the more common cravings. A very rare but documented pica is kitchen cleanser and sponges. Linda would shake Comet on a sponge, sit down in front of the TV, and nibble the sponge until it was gone. She had been doing this for years, and no one remembers just when or how it started. But it was something from which she had to withdraw, along with the other drugs.

After she had completely withdrawn from the drugs, Linda needed time to adjust to a new lifestyle. Every activity was an effort for her, making even chores as simple as getting out of bed a stress for her. Tom Mahairas suggested she go to TLC. At the time there were no residents. Only the director and his wife, Bill and Barbara Shaw, were there.

Linda was the first and only woman ever to become a resident at TLC, spending four weeks there. The first week the Shaws took care of her. The second, her mother and step-father, Evelyn and John came. John said, "I'll go, but nobody's going to push their religious beliefs on me!" This was respected. It was a time when Evelyn bonded with her daughter. The third week Linda's brother Jimmy stayed with her. And the last week, Billy was there. Linda received special care and attention the entire month, but she told Billy, "I liked it best when you were with me."

Linda was baptized a short time after she came home. God truly had transformed her. Without God's strength, she never would have gotten off drugs. She was a new person, with life and a vibrancy she never had before. Linda was added to the ranks of sinners changed by the grace of God. In giving her testimony to the church, she said, "When I didn't know God, I prayed to Him and asked Him to send me an angel. Four months later he answered my prayer. An angel knocked on my door, in the form of my husband."

Still, something was missing in the Schneider home. Billy's return had brought life into the home. Linda still was very quiet, perhaps a bit depressed. In fact, Linda was sick, her body giving out because of the years of abuse. Sometimes Billy would come home and find that Linda had spent much of the day in bed. Young Billy needed something else as well. They were both drawing life from Billy. When he was home, the house came alive. When he cooked, everyone was happy. Little Billy especially would never miss a meal cooked by Dad.

Billy decided a dog might help, so he took Linda with him to the North Shore Animal League on Long Island. He looked up and down the aisles into each cage. In the last cage sat a black dog. Stuck on the cage was a sign, "Last day for Charles. Absolutely no good with kids or cats." Billy took one look and said, "Charles, you're coming home with me." Linda was horrified. She was not enthused about a dog, but had agreed to a small one. This dog was the size of a German Shepherd. Billy learned later that he was a Belgian sheepdog. Totally black except for a white star on his chest, he was beautiful. As they neared home, Billy looked in the rearview mirror. In the darkness he could hardly see this new family member. It was five minutes to twelve. "Midnight," Billy said. "What a good name! Well, Midnight, here's your new family and your new home."

Midnight became a beloved part of the family. It didn't take Linda long to become attached to him. He endeared himself to her when he rescued Oodie the cat one night. Midnight was restless, constantly bothering Linda with his whining. Finally she woke Billy up. "What is wrong with him?" Billy got up to investigate, and Midnight kept going to the window and whining. At last Billy looked down, and there on the fire escape little Oodie sat shaking. She had somehow fallen out the window and into the rainy night and couldn't get back in.

Billy asked Linda to take Midnight for his daily walks in the park. The walks gave her a reason to leave the apartment. Little Billy, who was fourteen or fifteen at the time, found a playmate in Midnight. But the pet bonded most tightly with Billy himself. He truly became a best friend for Billy.

CHAPTER 17

Going Home

Linda had been on some form of drug since she was fourteen, and for eighteen years she rarely missed a daily dose of Methadone. She did not know what it felt like to be herself, free from chemical dependence. For the past ten or fifteen years, she had spent more time in a nightgown, in a zombie-like state, than in any other outfit.

Tremendous changes must have taken place in her body as she withdrew not only from drugs, but also from the poisonous habit of eating sponges and kitchen cleanser. Linda looked more alive, was more outgoing, and she began to make friends at church. For the first time in years she had a relationship with her mom. "I've got my daughter back," Evelyn would say happily.

But the damage had been done. Linda's liver had worked overtime to try to discard the poisons that had been poured into her body and cirrhosis had set in. For years she had gone without proper medical care. The Methadone likely had masked symptoms so that she did not feel the destruction going on inside.

Withdrawal complete, Linda began to feel sick. She did not have much energy, and her abdomen began to bloat. At last, she sought much needed medical attention.

Along with other tests, her doctor suggested HIV. Linda was in a high-risk category. She had assumed for some time that she was positive, and, in fact, often would jokingly say, "I have AIDS." It came as no surprise to her when, in 1990, she found she was HIV positive. She looked at Billy and read something in his face. She said with concern, "I know what you're thinking – that I got it from you. But it doesn't matter. For a long time I thought that I gave it to you. But it still doesn't matter." He held her close as they reassured one another. Who could know just when or how either she or Billy had become positive?

One day during that summer, Billy came home to find Linda in bed. "What's the matter?" he asked her.

"I have cancer!" she replied. She had been to the doctor to receive the results of a test.

Billy thought about this for a few moments. Then he asked, "Aside from the fact that you heard the diagnosis of cancer today, how do you feel differently?"

"I guess I don't," she responded.

"Then get out of bed!"

Billy is a person who never gives up, and he refused to let Linda do so, either. He wanted her to go on living. Early on he had made a decision that neither HIV, nor any other illness for that matter, was going to govern his life. He wanted Linda to do the same.

By mid-1992, Linda was spending more and more time undergoing tests and treatments, including bone marrow and other biopsies because of falling blood counts. Treatment for the cervical cancer had been discussed, but with so much deterioration of her liver, chemotherapy was not a viable option. She was given supportive treatments – blood and platelet transfusions. They did little to change her condition. Life began ebbing out of Linda's little body, almost as though it was saying, "Enough is enough."

From June on, Linda was in the hospital frequently. Billy began spending less time working and more time caring for her. He found that being in the hospital does not mean all your needs as a patient automatically will be met. He learned to be a nurse himself as she weakened, tenderly bathing and cleaning her up, grateful to be able to help her with basic activities of daily living.

Her abdomen continued to fill with fluid because of the liver failure. It became necessary to drain this fluid for Linda's comfort. Every day or two, she began to beg to be drained. The doctors would come in with a large needle and pierce her abdominal wall, allowing the fluid to drain into a bottle.

Billy knew Linda was dying. He treasured these final few years he had with her. What a difference from the first years of marriage! The vows spoken in confusion in 1972 were coming true in 1992 – "until death us do part." Yes, God had heard those vows. And God was faithful. He had allowed Billy to truly love his wife. He had given Linda peace. After all the years of sin, of drugs, of spitting in God's face, He still had touched Billy and Linda with His amazing grace.

On December 2 they celebrated their twentieth wedding anniversary. Billy filled the hospital room with balloons and flowers. After fourteen years of separation, Billy had come home. Now, three years later, Linda was going home.

On December 8, 1992, at 8:05 p.m., surrounded by friends and with Billy at her side, Linda met her Savior face to face. Several people sat with Billy, including Jimmy and his girlfriend Denise, Billy's mom Helen, Linda's friend from church Martha Kinsley, and other relatives and friends. In that hospital room they were witnesses to a spirit being ushered into eternal life. Linda had been comatose for several days. Now she was very restless. Billy sat stroking her, saying gently "Let go, baby. Just let go." Suddenly, Linda's body came right up off the bed, as she, still in comatose state, let out a great cry. Billy ran out and fetched the doctor, who came in and sedated her. Moments later, and in absolute calm, Linda's spirit was gone, freed from the prison of a ravaged body.

Billy had to deal with funeral arrangements. He had never known just how complicated that was. Deciding on a funeral home, picking out a casket, the clothes Linda should wear, having her hair done, notifying people, planning a wake and a burial. One by one these tasks were accomplished.

Billy purchased a cemetery lot. The manager said to him, "I have only two spots available," and he showed him the first one. It did not suit Billy. As he brought him to the second lot, Billy thought, This looks familiar! Two plots over, Alan Rosenfeld had been buried just one month earlier! "Linda, you're gonna' love this!" Billy cried. Linda had loved Alan. Now Billy could imagine the guy buried between them telling them, "Quiet down! After all, this is a cemetery, don't you know?"

The funeral was planned, but a storm was brewing. Two major upper-air systems collided, bringing the coldest weather and the worst storm to hit New York City in eighty-five years. In spite of this, at least two hundred people attended the wake on Friday and the funeral Saturday. Linda's mom and step-dad came in from Long Island. Thirty minutes after they crossed the Throg's Neck Bridge, it was closed to traffic.

Was God still in charge? Billy knew that He was, without question. He had calmed the raging storms in Billy's life. He could be trusted with this storm. At the wake, Pastor Tom began to speak. Suddenly Linda's step-father John got up. A quiet man and one who vowed he would not be bent by anyone's religion, he stood with tears streaming down his face. He interrupted Tom, and, turning to face the audience, said, "I came from a small town in Idaho. I have never experienced this type of love anywhere. Not in the small town, not in the city. If this is due to Jesus, I need to accept Him right now!" Kneeling at the foot of their daughter's casket, both John and Evelyn accepted the Lord. From death to life! What a moment on earth! And what a party in heaven, as Linda witnessed the spiritual homecoming of her parents!

Was their experience real? The next day Billy overheard Evelyn say words she had never spoken in her entire life. "Jesus helped me through this," she told someone who asked about her grief.

What a family time this was. Sunday's service was dedicated to Linda. Billy and Jimmy gave testimonies, and Pastor Tom announced that Billy was going to come on staff at TLC. Jimmy sang "Calvary's Love," a song he dedicated "to Linda, and her new life."

"There's a yearning in all our lives, that only Jesus satisfies," he sang with feeling. Linda's mom and step-dad spent their first Sunday as believers at the Manhattan Bible Church hearing testimonies to God's ever-amazing grace.

As difficult as the past months had been, Billy still could say, "God gave me the best Christmas present ever when he took Linda home."

CHAPTER 19

Changes

Billy no longer had a heart for business. He had made enough money. He used to say, "Lord, stop this! I don't need any more!" when he was blessed with yet another job, yet another check. He felt God was calling him into ministry. He asked Tom about being on staff at Transformation Life Center. Arrangements were made for him to move there, and Billy sold his business to a general contractor.

As he was getting ready to leave the apartment in New York that had been his home for the past three years, Billy knocked on his neighbor's door. "Nilda," he said, "I'm ready to leave. I just have one question for you. Do you know that I'm a Christian?" His aim in life was to share his faith, and he wanted to know if his neighbors had heard the gospel from him.

With tears in her eyes, Nilda responded, "Oh, yes, Billy. Everyone here knows you love the Lord!" Only then was Billy able to leave. Now he says, "If I am asked to give money to someone who wants to go on the mission field, I would like first to visit their neighbors and ask them if they have heard the gospel from these prospective missionaries. Only if they have a clear testimony with their neighbors would I consider supporting them!"

One of Billy's first duties after arriving at TLC was to travel to a church in Pembroke, Ontario, Canada. This church had been supporting TLC for years, and they needed a progress report. In January 1993, Billy boarded a plane, but he nearly created a disaster on this, his first speaking engagement. He fell asleep while waiting for a plane change in Syracuse and missed his next flight. Don Healey, who was to pick him up, had to travel many miles to the airport. When Billy finally arrived, immigration officers were inclined to send him home because he couldn't tell them exactly where he was headed or who was going to pick him up. He was beginning to feel a bit desperate, when suddenly he saw Don through the glass doors. He was still there, after all that time! God surely came to his aid.

In February God gave Billy an opportunity to speak at Moody Founder's Week. Sometime earlier a scheduled speaker had canceled, and Tom asked Joe Stowell, president of Moody Bible Institute, if he could bring Billy. Joe was thrilled to have him come, especially since he already had known another TLC graduate, Billy's friend Alan Rosenfeld, and been so excited about his testimony he wrote of his death in Moody Monthly magazine.

At Moody, alongside such Christian giants as Chuck Colson, E. V. Hill, and Joni Erickson Tada, Billy was able share his testimony in front of thousands. Even so, Billy was the only speaker to be given a standing ovation as he shared both street stories and the greatness of God's unchanging love in his life. He told them, "I'm still on pills. I take four a day – Matthew, Mark, Luke, and John. I'm on the Gos-pill!" With openness, he could say, "I may be HIV positive, but I don't focus on that. I focus instead on being JESUS-positive!"

Back at TLC, Billy's responsibilities were varied, including assisting the director, Jerry Carella. He remodeled one of the buildings into an apartment for himself. He counseled many of the residents. They needed someone who was street-wise and who would not be fooled by them. He usually could tell if a resident was in trouble. With his humor and wit, he kept things lively. He was a strong example to residents that change is possible. Billy's dog Midnight also became a favorite at camp. He could always sense a person's spirit, and he cheered up Billy in his times of distress. Now he did the same for the residents.

It soon became clear that God had other work for Billy to do. He was invited to speak in churches, prisons, schools. His message is a powerful one, warning students of the perils of drug use, illicit sex, and pornography. His messages to churches stirr them to evangelism. "Where were God's people when I was in prison, when I was on the streets and in great need?" he asks. Christians need to learn how to deal with issues such as AIDS, homosexuality, and drug addiction. After all, don't Christians have the only real answer to every problem and situation encountered in life? AIDS, drugs and sexual problems are not too big, or too nasty, to be dealt with by the Church. Billy is living testimony to this.

CHAPTER 20

Sarah's Story

Billy was invited to Normal, Illinois, to speak at the Illinois State University campus in September 1994. A great deal of advertising and publicity preceded his visit. Jerry McCorkle, the pastor who brought him to Normal, put progressive ads in the paper. The first day the ad read:

"Mom, I met a guy named Billy."

The next day more information was added,

"Mom, I met a guy named Billy . . . but he's HIV positive."

You can be sure that got the attention of every mom who had a child on campus! It continued:

"Mom, I met a guy named Billy . . . but he's HIV positive . . . and he's been addicted to heroin for 22 years."

And continuing the next day:

"Mom, I met a guy named Billy . . . but he's HIV positive . . . and he's been addicted to heroin for 22 years . . . and he also spent 10 years in prison."

And finally a full page ad:

"MOM, I MET A GUY NAMED BILLY...
   BUT HE'S HIV POSITIVE...
      AND HE'S BEEN ADDICTED TO HEROIN FOR 22 YEARS...
      AND HE ALSO SPENT 10 YEARS IN PRISON...
         BUT WHAT HE SAID CHANGED MY LIFE FOREVER."

Just before he left New York for Normal, Billy got a haircut, and his buddy Jerry Carella razzed him: "How come you got such a stupid-looking haircut? They'll think you're a freak!" Billy couldn't wait to show Jerry the press reports: "In his jeans and cowboy boots, a white T-shirt and fashionable hair cut. . . ." Billy was well-received on campus, at the local high school, and in the church.

But on this trip, it wasn't the hype, it wasn't the newspaper articles, it wasn't speaking at the church, and it wasn't riding horseback at midnight that impressed him most. These are not the things he talks about when he discusses his visit to Normal, Illinois. Instead he talks about a six-year-old girl whose innocent and childish devotion to him once again changed his life.

Billy was lonely. It had been almost two years since Linda had died. The wall he had built around his heart when he felt so rejected by his church family was still there. Being HIV positive and now single, the wall was even more pronounced. When Linda died, Billy's hope of having any future companionship seemed to die with her. How could he expect anyone to take on an intimate relationship with someone bearing the burden of HIV? He certainly was not open to more pain.

Billy's magnetic personality attracted many girls to flirt with him. But he was wary, knowing that getting his hopes up would lead only to more crushing pain. He had, in fact, tried letting the wall down several times during these lonely months, only to be hurt. It was one thing to have fun with Billy. It was quite another to think of marriage. Billy knew this. He restored the wall, but went on being "Billy" on the outside. Always happy, always loving the Lord, always with a joke and a twinkle in his eye. But on the inside there was a pain no one could see.

God had a surprising way of dealing with Billy's pain. He sent six-year-old Sarah McCorkle into his life. Sarah absolutely fell in love with Billy. She followed him everywhere. She sat on his lap, she hugged him, she kissed him, she tweaked his hair. She wanted to sit by him at mealtimes. Billy was pleased by her affection for him, but also uncomfortable. Should he put up barriers and push her away? She certainly wouldn't understand. And what must her parents be thinking? Did they have unspoken fears? If you get too close to a wall like Billy's, either you get hurt or the wall comes down. And since Sarah was unaware and innocent, it was Billy who needed to make a decision about the wall. God was beginning to go to work.

Once God had Billy's attention, He said to him. "Take that wall down!" It was kind of a progressive message from God, sort of like the advertising hype that went before Billy's appearance on campus. God continued like this: "Take that wall down! I'm going to send people into your life to love you." And continuing, "Did you forget that I love you? That I touched you? Remember what you preach about Jesus touching the lepers. The demonic. Take it down, Billy. Otherwise you won't be able to let in the people I'm going to send your way."

Billy and God were in a wrestling match. God knew what Billy needed, and he was not going to let Billy live behind that wall any longer. But Billy was stubborn. "God, I've just been hurt too much!" God continued to work through Sarah. No one knew of the inner battle. This was Billy's and God's war. God knew a great deal that Billy did not know at that moment. He was moving, and the wall was simply in the way. It was an issue of trust. Was Billy willing to trust God? The wall seemed so logical and practical to Billy. It protected him from others, and others from him. It was comforting as a hiding place. He could look out, but no one could look in. It was his own security system. But God wanted to be Billy's security.

Ironically, Billy had been quoting a verse from Proverbs for some time: "He who finds a wife finds what is good, and receives favor from the Lord" (Proverbs 18:22 NIV). He would say that God gave him this verse, yet he did not believe the verse was truly meant for him. In his own corny way, he would make a joke of it. Friends saw him in Home Depot one day, and he put on a little charade of looking desperately for something. When they asked him what he was doing, he replied, "I'm looking for a wife. I thought Home Depot might have one," and then he quoted the verse. But in his heart it was no joke. Billy did want a wife. He desperately needed companionship, but he faced a great dilemma: how could he expect anyone to deliberately risk exposure to HIV? He couldn't bear to ask that of anyone. A wife seemed an impossible dream.

God was pleading gently with Billy to become vulnerable. He had allowed himself to be vulnerable to God in the past, when God had urged him to go back to Linda. God seemed to be saying, "I did give you that verse! Don't mock me with it!"

Billy also thought of the amazing changes that had taken place in his life since he had taken another wall down seven years earlier – the wall that had kept him from eternal life, from a personal relationship with Jesus Christ. It was the wall behind which he had lived in misery and wallowed in drug addiction for so many years, the wall he could have taken down long before he did, but stubbornly kept in place. It was the wall he kept up when Tom Mahairas shared the gospel with him. He remembered the tremendous joy that flowed when he took that wall down on the day he trusted that Jesus Christ meant what He said, "Come to me, all you who are weary and burdened, and I will give you rest." This was the day Billy Schneider jumped into the arms of Jesus. He had discovered that day that God was not a liar.

Billy gave in. God won once again. He knew what He was about. What God had in store for Billy was just around the corner, and now the wall was out of the way. God didn't attack Billy or send a preacher. He didn't scold. He sent a child who in innocent love walked right through Billy's wall.

Sarah painted a picture of Billy after he preached in their church. It is a water color stick man with an ear-to-ear grin and arms and hands open wide, done in cheerful blues and greens. The picture hangs on our wall now. Billy asked Sarah, "Why did you just draw me?" since there was a whole team from New York with them. "Because I love you," the child told him. And in her innocence she led Billy to submit his protective wall to God.

Sarah sobbed uncontrollably as Billy was leaving. The team stopped at the church/school to say good-bye. Sarah came out of her classroom for a moment, but when she was taken back into her classroom, she cried so hard that the teacher sent someone to fetch Billy, and he came into her classroom to console her.

Billy wrote a poem for Sarah on his way home from Normal. In that simple communication, Billy's heart was laid open to begin to let others in. It shows how immediately he understood God's message and messenger.

I saw her,
She saw me,
She didn't see
I was HIV

I saw within
Her eyes of brown
A wall of fear
Just tumble down.

A fear I built
From a painful trial
But what remains
Is her sweet smile.

A smile so pure
A touch so tender
A human being
I'll always remember.

Thank you Sarah
For helping me
To go on living
With HIV

And thank you Lord
For what you did
A mold was broken
When you formed this kid.

I am told this poem graces Sarah's wall. She is now eight years old, and at Christmas time last year I had the privilege of meeting her. She was shy and quiet, hardly remembering the Billy of the poem. Oh, to be like that! Letting God use her and not being conscious of it. She has no idea. But I, Billy's wife, say with Billy, "Thank you, Sarah!"

CHAPTER 21

Enter Joanne

I wonder what I might have thought as a high school senior had I known that my future husband was at that very time a fourteen-year-old punk, roaming the streets of New York City, smoking, investigating drugs, getting himself into trouble, a boy who already had spent a night in jail?

I'm glad I didn't know. I imagine I would have tried to manipulate life had I been cursed with such knowledge. Rather, I am thankful that God was in charge of my life. He was the one Who led me through all the confusing years to the point of meeting Billy, and, although confusing to me, my life was not confusing to God.

In a way my life had some parallels to Billy's. Although different in so many ways, the necessary threads were there, so that when we met, our lives were able to weave together intimately.

My family life was not at all like Billy's. Where his was not structured enough, mine was too structured. Where his was irreligious, mine was super-religious. He grew up in New York City, I was raised on a farm in Michigan. Billy stepped out into the world of the 1960s. He experienced the hippie era, the Vietnam era, the era of riots, of civil rebellion. I grew up nearly in total isolation from all of this. He was bold; I was afraid. He turned outward; I turned inward.

In spite of all that, there also were similarities. We both experienced shame. We both experienced confusion. There was in each of our lives loss, loneliness, and abuse. We each had a need to fix the pain. The frame was different, but the picture was similar. Each picture was filled with darkness. And into each picture came the beauty, the love, and the amazing light of Jesus Christ.

Yes, my life had been filled with darkness. My feelings toward God had vacillated between terror and indifference. But God had worked in my life in such a way as to convince me that "indeed, I am for you" (Ezekiel 36:9, NKJ), and that "If God be for me, who can be against me?" (Romans 8:31, paraphrased). He had convinced me (finally) that no matter what had been done to me, I was still a sinner myself. Then He showed me how He loves sinners. He brought forgiveness into my life. I was forgiven, so I could begin to forgive others. It was love on God's part, changing the picture, no matter how it had begun, no matter who had splattered their paint on it. Somehow, when God's Son shines through, the scene becomes beautiful.

Now, just two months after Sarah walked through the wall around Billy's heart, our eyes met. God had prepared both of us for that meeting at an inner-city mission in Grand Rapids, Michigan.

Bjon, a young man I had known since he was a child, was at Transformation Life Center. He had been addicted to drugs since age thirteen, and so far nothing had worked to free him. I received a message from him that he would be in Grand Rapids with a team from TLC and would be sharing his testimony at the Mel Trotter Mission on Friday, November 11, 1994. I wanted to see Bjon's eyes with my own, to see if this place called Transformation Life Center was working.

As I walked into the Mission, I noticed two people. One was a friend. Two seats away from him sat a woman, the only one besides me in this men's mission. There was an empty seat between them, so I took it. The meeting was just about to begin. Soon it was Bjon's turn, and I was thrilled with what I heard and saw. His eyes were clear, his testimony strong, even though he stuttered as usual. It was still Bjon, but he was looking good.

Then Billy Schneider got up. I had heard him before at "Saturday Night," an alternative service at Calvary Church, designed to meet the needs of people who would be uncomfortable in a traditional Sunday morning service. Billy's testimony had moved me. I even had thought of trying to meet him because I was interested in the changes God had made in his life. But I remembered seeing him in the parking lot at Calvary, surrounded by girls all trying to get his attention. That did NOT interest me!

As he spoke about how he had heard the word "Jump!" thrcc times in his life, the woman next to me began to weep. Billy's story had touched an area of pain in her life. She continued weeping during the altar call, so I finally asked if she would like me to go with her to the altar and pray. Yes, she would. How was I to know that God had a purpose beyond her need? Not that this woman was unimportant to Him, but in being available for her need I became available for God to do something in my life as well. I prayed with her as she wept and cried out in her pain.

At last we got up from our knees, she partially comforted, I with eyes red from weeping with her. As I got up, my eyes looked straight into Billy Schneider's eyes, those twinkling brown eyes that always attracted people. They were so open to his soul, it was as though you could look in and see the joy in his spirit. He looked into my teary eyes and said, "You have such sensitive eyes!" We really did not meet that night. He did not know my name. Yet in that moment of something passed between us that each of us felt. As I walked out of the mission to another event, I said to my friends, "I met Billy Schneider tonight." And Billy? Well, he dogged Bjon: "Who is that woman?"

"Jo Jo Jo Joanne," Bjon stuttered in response.

"Joanne who?" Billy demanded.

"Jo Jo Jo Joanne Martin."

"Do you have her phone number?" Billy pressed. And Bjon balked, becoming protective. Billy used his position as staff member at TLC, and said, "Gimme her phone number, Bjon, or else it's dishes for two weeks when we get back to TLC!" Bjon gave in.

Not that Billy knew what he would do with my number. Just what was this going on inside him? The next day he did nothing. But on Sunday, he spoke at a church near Grand Rapids, and the pastor offered him his study in which to relax before speaking again in the evening. Casual and comfortable as Billy can become, he put his feet up on the pastor's desk. From that position, the phone seemed to be staring at him. Should I? he thought. Why not? So he fished the number Bjon had given him out of his pocket and dialed it. The phone rang, once, twice, three, four times, then he heard "You know what to do with these machines..." So to a mechanical messenger he said, "You may think it's strange, hearing from me, but this is Billy Schneider. I am speaking tonight at Grand Valley Baptist Church, and, well, I just wondered if you might be interested in coming."

When I arrived home from work a short time later and picked up the message, I knew immediately this was no missionary call. Billy's first statement had given me a clue. Somehow I knew I was to go. But I certainly did not want to go alone to a strange church to meet a strange person. I had no idea what to expect. I'd feel more comfortable with a friend along, but with only an hour to spare I couldn't find a friend to go with me.

I thought of the woman at the mission. She was a searching soul. Perhaps hearing another message would help her. I located her, and she was thrilled to go. Little did I know that Barbara had developed an infatuation for Billy, and all the way to the church she was telling me what she would like to do with him. What had I gotten myself into? Help, Lord! I cried inwardly as we neared the church. I was determined not to be embarrassed to be with her, and we walked into the church just as the service was about to begin. This way Billy did not know I was there, and I was relieved to see some friends there.

I tried to avoid making eye contact with Billy as he spoke. But about halfway through his talk, our eyes met anyway. Billy stopped speaking! Billy at a loss for words! What was this? Billy looked to his friend Paul Fleming, a singer who is in ministry with Billy. "Paul, do you have a song for us?" Paul got up, unsure of what was happening. This was not in the plan. There were only two people in this room who knew what this was about. One was uncomfortable, the other not sure whether to laugh or be alarmed. Paul walked to the front of the church and said, "No, Billy, I don't." Let down by his friend, Billy nevertheless had enough time to recover, and he went on. And no one seemed to be the wiser.

Afterward, Billy was surrounded by people. I was nervous and didn't know what to expect. I certainly did not rush to where Billy was greeting others. I stayed right where I was, thankful for the friends God knew I needed to have there.

At last Billy broke away and came to where I was.

"Joanne!" he cried, "you have to help me! I don't know what's going on. This has never happened to me before!"

Well, I wasn't sure exactly what he meant, but it was clear to both of us that whatever he was feeling inside was different from anything he had previously experienced. This was not a bad sign. I did not want to be just another victim of a parking-lot flirtation.

We needed at least a few minutes to talk. But there was Barbara, sticking to Billy like glue. At last I said, "Barbara, I need to talk to Billy. Why don't you get some refreshments?"

She got the hint, and off she went, only to return a few minutes later to announce, "Billy, I want our picture taken together. There's someone here with a camera." She never had a clue what was really going on, and months later, after we were married, she sent Billy a copy of the picture along with a gushing letter.

What was so different about what was happening to Billy? Eventually he understood and explained it to me. He had met my spirit that night at the Mel Trotter Mission. I'm a "spirit" person anyway, so this was not unusual. My spirit senses the spirit in others very quickly, but for Billy, this was different. When he met a woman he noticed her physically first, but not so this time, and he couldn't figure it out. Later he said to me, "I'm glad you're pretty. When I met you, I didn't even notice your body, and that was what had never happened to me before." And of course, we know, because it is a saying, that beauty is in the eye of the beholder.

I believe this was very much connected to what had happened about two months earlier in Billy's life. His spirit was no longer imprisoned by his wall and could operate freely.

The rest of the team returned to New York. Billy stayed on in Grand Rapids for the next week and a half. God provided time for Billy to get acquainted with someone significant to him. Others planned changes in his ministry, including a move to Grand Rapids from New York. But God had an ultimate plan in mind.

CHAPTER 22

Joanne and HIV

The first hurdle we confronted in our relationship was the HIV issue. "Why me, why us, Lord?" I wondered. Everything else had to be put on hold while both of us wrestled with it. To have or not to have a relationship was a matter that hinged on HIV. To be "just friends" never entered Billy's mind. Someone quoting Proverbs 18:22 on his first date left little room for speculation as to where this relationship was heading. ("Whoso findeth a wife findeth a good thing, and obtaineth favor of the Lord." KJV) I had to think immediately of this relationship in terms of marriage.

As a nurse, I am very conscious of contamination, of blood and body fluids. "Universal precautions" are part of my everyday life. HIV was something to think of in panic if I accidentally stuck myself with a needle. When I began nursing in the 1960s, there was life in the blood. "Aids" were what we called the persons who helped us nurses finish our day's work. In the 1990s, however, it seems is death in the blood. AIDS is a disease, not a title. Patient care includes "handle with care" in a way that earlier had not been known.

I did not know anyone who was HIV positive or who had AIDS. Oh, I knew OF people, but that is entirely different from being in a close relationship with someone who is marked by the plague of the 20th Century. I had no understanding of what it might feel like to be positive, living with AIDS, and facing death from AIDS.

So what would move me to enter into an intimate relationship with someone who is HIV positive? How could I walk a fine line between nurture, needs and precautions? Were gloves to become a part of tenderness, something to wear when touching my spouse? Would I need to spend my days disinfecting and sterilizing? In my wildest dreams, or nightmares, I had not imagined bringing this dreaded disease into my home, let alone into my bed.

"Oh God! Help!" I knew that Billy Schneider would not just go away. And I was very attracted to him. I could not say no just because of HIV. I had felt from the beginning that God was involved. So this was an issue for God, not me. I felt helpless to protect myself should I marry Billy. After all, I could not see that tiny virus. How could I prevent its invasion? How could I avoid absolute paranoia once into the situation? I couldn't! No more than I could add hairs to my head. But God can see what I never will see. When I had trusted Him for eternal life, at the same time I put my trust in His care for my earthly life. Could I not then entrust my body to Him for protection and let Him monitor where that virus went?

God knew my fears, and He had an answer for me – immediately. I had been reading the *One-Minute Bible™ for Students* as a short bedtime devotional. On November 19, just eight days after meeting Billy and at a time when I was praying specifically about the HIV issue, I read this passage:

> Now there was in Damascus a believer named Ananias. The Lord spoke to him in a vision, calling "Ananias!"
> "Yes, Lord!" he replied. And the Lord said, "Go over to Straight Street and find the house of a man named Judas and ask there for Saul of Tarsus. He is praying to me right now, for I have shown him in a vision of a man named Ananias coming in and laying his hands on him so he can see again!
> "But Lord," exclaimed Ananias, "I have heard about the terrible things this man has done to the believers in Jerusalem! And we hear that he has warrants with him from the chief priests, authorizing him to arrest every believer in Damascus!"
> But the Lord said, "Go and do what I say. For Saul is my chosen instrument to take my message to the nations and before kings, as well as to the people of Israel.
> So Ananias went over and found Saul and laid his hands on him and said, "Brother Saul, the Lord Jesus, who appeared to you on the road, has sent me so that you may be filled with the Holy Spirit and get your sight back."   Acts 19:10-15,17 TLB

To Ananias, Saul was deadly. He did not want to go to this man, much less touch him. His reply to God was something like this: "What? You want me to touch him? You know he's deadly! No way, Lord! Not me!" But God said, "Yes, you lay your hands on him. Touch him! He is my chosen instrument. And besides, I've already told him you're coming." And in this way Ananias also was God's instrument – chosen to give Saul a healing touch.

To me, Billy carried the potential to be deadly. And I was saying the same thing. "Touch him? No way, Lord. He's deadly!" But God already had chosen Billy to go and tell others what great and mighty things He had done for him. Now He was urging me, "Trust me. I know what I am doing. Don't be afraid to touch Billy! Go to him! He is My chosen instrument. And he's already expecting you!"

Well! This could not have been more clear. In His grace and goodness, God knew there was something in this book that would help me, and months before had guided me to pick up the *One-Minute Bible*™ *for Students.*

Yes, Billy is carrying a deadly virus, one that could without a doubt be passed on to me and kill me. And no, I don't believe that my touch was meant to heal Billy of HIV. That was not God's message to me. Not that I don't believe God could heal Billy if he wished. But if Billy were healed, perhaps his message to students would not be so powerful. Imagine, in his attempt to warn young people of the grim reality of AIDS, Billy saying, "I was HIV positive, but I'm not any more." This could dilute Billy's powerful message of the deadliness of wrong choices, leading students to believe that they, too, could carelessly make wrong choices, since they, too, just might be healed.

I believe that, just like Saul, Billy is God's chosen instrument to preach the gospel to many. His message to students is not just about making wise choices regarding drug use, sexual activity, pornography, tobacco, and wrong attitudes. His ultimate desire is to bring them the good news that Jesus Christ is the answer for each of life's problems, that He is the one wise choice to make, with results both in this life and for eternity. I could not doubt God's message to me.

Besides this, God allowed me to speak with two women, both of them nurses, whose husbands also are HIV positive. One married her husband knowing he was positive, the other had been married for some time before they found he was positive. They both told me of things they did to protect themselves. Neither of them has become HIV positive.

Neither God's message to me nor the experiences of others assured me that I would not become HIV positive myself. They did tell me two things, however. The first gave me assurance of God's direction with regard to HIV. The latter told me that it is possible to be in a marriage relationship with an HIV-infected spouse without becoming infected myself.

Billy and I do not want anyone to get the wrong idea. We never would encourage someone to do lightly what we have done. We know there are and will be others who face choices such as Billy's and mine. What counsel would we give them? We would want to know first and foremost where both of them stand with God. Have they asked God without manipulation what He wants for them? Are they willing to accept His answer? Are they aware of the risks and willing to face them? Are they realistic about the fact that God does not promise miraculous cures, or miraculous protection? Are they realistic about the reality of a death that could be very painful? Are they willing to become educated about HIV and about protective measures, perhaps including the denial of physical desires? All this in addition to the usual concerns about entering a marriage relationship.

Furthermore, we never will endorse the idea of "safe sex" because of our situation. Safe sex seems to be a term used to "get away with" wrong sex; in other words, sex outside a heterosexual marriage. God has much to say about marriage and its sanctity. In His first mention of marriage, He said "...they will become one flesh." (Genesis 2:24, NIV) There is something mystical about this statement. A physician friend recently told me that he has read that when a bone marrow transplant is needed, researchers (according to one article) are finding that the spouse often is the most compatible donor. There seems to be a special blending of flesh within the marriage union. In that blend, it would seem that there is protection as well. God has not promised that I won't become HIV positive. He has not promised a life of ease or a life free from sorrow or pain. He has, however, promised to be with us. Billy and I are careful to protect me from the virus, and Billy from the illnesses of others. But we place our trust in God, knowing that our lives are in His hands.

Several years ago, I took Philippians 4:13 for my life verse: "I can do everything through Him who gives me strength. NIV" By nature I am a fearful person. But Christ has given me a new nature, including His strength. and I know that He will not leave me in my time of greatest need, which may yet be coming.

CHAPTER 23

A Jump of Faith

With the HIV issue answered so plainly, Billy and I now had other matters with which to deal. Our relationship had been unusual from the start. We both knew that it was God's plan for us to meet. We both had been praying about a mate. Billy had taken Proverbs 18:22 as a promise from God.

For the past year I had begun asking God about whether He had a husband for me. I had learned through a disastrous marriage earlier that a husband could not cure loneliness or other areas of pain in my life. God had used the dark circumstances surrounding a divorce to show me that He had the answer to the problems that had led me to seek marriage the first time. A time of healing followed that difficult era of my life. Now, fourteen years later, I felt God might be waiting for me to ask Him whether His plans for my future might include a husband. "You have not, because you ask not" came to mind. My prayer went like this: "Lord, if you have a husband for me, please, please, make him be emotionally and spiritually alive!" Unless it was God's plan, I did not want a husband. But if God did have marriage in mind for me, I did not think it could hurt to put in a specific request.

After I began to pray in this way, several men asked me for dates. After fourteen years and no dates, was God telling me something? Was one of these men an answer to my prayer? I tried them out. These were all "nice" men, but I found there was just no "zing." I told a friend that although I had met many single men, most of them were "dead men walking." Certainly none fit my request of God.

Then I met Billy. For anyone who knows him, that's all I need to say. For those of you who don't, all I can say is, "You're missing something." His wit, his humor, his testimony of God's amazing grace in his life, his witness to this in every conversation, and his zeal for living all made him fit my prayer. The "zing" was unmistakable.

I first was attracted to Billy because of his love for his Savior. It is genuine and obvious. Then there was another factor. I had said, on occasion, "I wouldn't mind being married. It's the courtship thing I can't deal with." Billy never really asked me for a date. He just asked me to marry him! Actually, I rather liked that – I immediately knew what we needed to work toward. It moved us right out of the "let's just be friends and have fun" zone. In Billy's life, there was a clear urgency. He felt he was under a death sentence. He did not have time for courtship.

I went to my pastor, who knew both of us. He said to me, "Joanne, go to New York. See Billy in his own environment before you make a decision."

Things were moving so quickly that events seemed out of my control, yet I had a secure sense they were in God's control, and His plan was about to unfold. Billy was to move to Michigan in January. I needed to go to New York immediately if I were to follow Pastor Ed's advice. Billy and I decided I should visit over the New Year's weekend. By this time Billy already had asked me to marry him many times. "Why not?" he would say. "Give me reasons not to marry me!" God had already dealt with us about the HIV issue. Whenever Billy asked this question, my mind seemed to go blank. Why shouldn't I marry him? Yet, he was a man I hardly knew.

I needed a definite answer from God. If Billy was God's choice for me, His answer to my prayer, I needed to know for sure. Settling the HIV issue was not enough. Having prayed for a husband was not enough. Now I needed to know if Billy was to be my husband. I decided to be specific with God. I asked Him to give me the answer I needed about Billy through this trip. "Lord," I prayed one week before my trip was to begin, "if you do not want me to marry Billy, do not let me get to New York. There are many ways You can prevent this."

That entire week I spent my days waiting for accidents, snowstorms, or other disasters. But nothing happened, and on Friday I climbed aboard the US Air jet at the Kent County International Airport, realizing that if God were going to stop this trip now it would inconvenience other people, or even put them in jeopardy

We took off as scheduled. We landed in Pittsburgh as scheduled. We took off from Pittsburgh as scheduled. Well, Lord? My heart beat faster as we neared LaGuardia. Our flight was scheduled to land at 9:59 p.m. The audacity of US Air! Couldn't they have said 10 p.m.? Well, not only did we land safely, we pulled in to the terminal gate at precisely 9:59 p.m. Now all that remained was meeting Billy.

On this last leg of the journey, I sat with a young man who was going to be met by his fiancé. As we got off the plane together, we both wondered if our special persons would be there to greet us. Sure enough, his fiancé was there, smiling and excited. But where was Billy? He was nowhere to be seen. Whew! Was I deflated! Had God brought me this far only to leave me stranded in a strange city, one of the world's largest? This was no way to answer my prayer, was it? With some apprehension, I moved along toward the luggage pick-up area. As I stood quietly waiting for my bag, not knowing how to feel, suddenly a rose appeared in front of my face, followed by an arm. I turned and there he was! God had answered my prayer! The significance of that moment hardly sunk in to me until later as we drove the eighty-five miles to Transformation Life Center, where Billy was living. God had said, "Marry Billy." At this moment, my life was forever changed. I felt acute tension and absolute peace at the same time.

As we drove out of the airport in Billy's 1987 Saab Turbo convertible with the top down (It was mid-winter, but Billy was so excited about my experiencing his car!), I knew I was faced with a dilemma. On the one hand, I was following my pastor's advice. I needed to learn some things about Billy before making a decision about marriage. On the other hand, I had asked God specifically for an answer about marrying Billy, and He had. So I needed to get answers, and I had received an answer. That left me with one more question: what, and when, do I tell Billy? He knew why I was coming to New York, but he didn't know about my specific request. Billy settled my confusion by asking me once again to marry him as we drove to TLC. I should have known. I told him the story, and he was thrilled that God was so interested in our situation. But it seemed that God was pushing us with an urgency. I began to understand this better as I understood Billy more.

And what did I learn about Billy? When I returned home, I said to Pastor Ed, "If I am treated half as well as Billy's dog is, I will be treated royally." Midnight had been with Billy through many of life's storms in the past five years, and they are special friends. In the times of loneliness, at the time of Linda's death, in dealing with the HIV issue, Midnight always was excited to be with Billy.

I learned more about Billy by experiencing TLC. I met many of Billy's friends, both at TLC and at the Manhattan Bible Church during their New Year's Eve party. I saw how genuinely they loved him. I heard from Tom Mahairas how Billy had cared for Linda during her sickness and death. I met a rough-looking Harley rider whom Billy had led to the Lord. He was a person many Christians would not have approached. I liked what I saw and heard.

I met Billy's mom, who did not yet know the Lord, and felt a relationship could develop between us. I sensed her moving toward me rather than pushing away as I feared she might.

I also learned that there were things that would likely need to change for me if I were married to Billy. He was quick and "New Yorkish" in his ways. His past made him think and behave differently than I did. I did not understand much of what it was like coming from the past he had. I didn't yet know much about that past. Although I was confident in God, there were still things that looked either difficult or impossible.

God was prepared for these doubts as well. I kept in mind my trip to New York, an answer to a specific prayer, and now God was going to prove to me that it was definitely His answer and not just a coincidence.

As I prepared to go home, God must have been chuckling. My flight was scheduled to leave LaGuardia midmorning. Billy and I were up early at TLC, eighty-five miles away. There a snowstorm raged – thick wet stuff that made driving hazardous. Everywhere there were cars off the road. Progress was slow, and it looked as though we would not make my flight. Billy said, "How can they be flying today?" We stopped to call the airport about trying to reschedule a flight from the small Stewart Airport much nearer TLC. Billy was assured that there was no problem with flights leaving LaGuardia, and no, there was no way for me to fly from Stewart. But now, after stopping to call and having to wait a long time to use the one pay phone, we knew I would miss my flight. This also meant missing work, as I was scheduled to come in straight from the airport at 3 p.m.

We finally arrived in New York to sunny skies and no snow on the ground. We took care of my work problem with a phone call, made arrangements for me to fly out at about 5 p.m., then set out to enjoy our bit of extra time together by sightseeing a New York City quieted by the holiday weekend. We rode around with the top down, enjoying an amazing January 2, 1995.

At the appropriate time we drove to the airport, only to be told there would be a slight delay in my flight. One hour, two hours and more rolled by. I was getting anxious. My flight from Pittsburgh left at 8:30, and here it was nearly 7 p.m. We spoke with the ticket agent, and he assured us that I would make it. In fact, he refused to allow me to board an additional flight that had been arranged and was leaving before my delayed flight. "You'll make it. They're just having a bit of a weather problem in Pittsburgh." There was nothing we could do but wait. Finally, near 8 p.m., my flight took off.

Once on board I found that there was no weather problem in Pittsburgh; rather, there had been a mechanical problem with the plane. They didn't want to tell us because a US Air plane had crashed very recently. Oh, boy. But at least we were on the way. And there was nothing anyone on board could do now.

Finally we touched down about the same time as my flight was scheduled to leave for Grand Rapids. I still had hopes of making it; however, near the terminal, the plane stopped. The precious moments ticked away. At last the pilot's voice cut through the silence. "Well, of all things! With all the trouble we've had, now there's a truck parked right in front of the plane, and we can't find the driver!" The frustration in the pilot's voice was apparent. I couldn't help but laugh at the humor of it all. This was God's way of letting me know that He was in charge of times and flights. I missed my plane once again, and now had to stay overnight in Pittsburgh. Finally, a day and a half late and a few dollars short, I arrived home. God must have known that in the months ahead I would need much reassurance from Him that marrying Billy was His plan.

In mid-January Billy was once again packing to move, this time from TLC to Michigan, where he could more effectively continue a speaking ministry. Billy had teamed up with a young man named Paul Fleming. Growing up in St. Maarten, Paul had been singing in his own church since age six. They made an effective duo, and when Billy spoke in public schools, Paul would sing for the students. Paul's voice always made the students want to hear more, and a rally would be arranged by a local church. A pizza party, a concert by Paul, and Billy would then tell the rest of his story, which could not be fully shared in the school – just Who was responsible for changing his life.

With Billy now in Grand Rapids, and without a permanent home, we both felt that it would be wise to marry as soon as possible. David and Annette Kok graciously gave Billy a bedroom during this time. Neither of us doubted God's plan for our lives. Again we spoke to Pastor Ed. He strongly urged premarital counseling first. We felt this was wise advice. And God did not let us down here either. We were introduced to just the right person to counsel us.

Billy wanted to be married on February 14, since this was such a special day to him. With clearance from my pastor, who also called Tom Mahairas, we decided to go ahead before we were finished with premarital counseling. We would continue the counseling as husband and wife. It made sense to us, and Pastor Ed agreed.

Now we faced another problem. My church had a rule that a couple must complete counseling before a pastor could marry them. So although Pastor Ed had approved, he could not perform the wedding. We decided that an appropriate place to be married was where we had met, at the Mel Trotter Mission. The pastor, Tom Layman, was agreeable, so arrangements were made. The mission residents were to be our guests. They got excited about the big event and scrubbed the sanctuary from top to bottom. We thought it would be an encouragement to them to know that their lives could be changed, especially since Billy's had been so much like their own. However, our friends began to hear of our plans and wanted to come. We decided that they could come if they wanted to, and we would have a "bring your own" reception.

On February 13 Tom Mahairas came to Grand Rapids. He called a meeting with both of us and with our counselor, Tim. "You can't do this!" he said. He was adamant.

I said, "Where were you when these plans were made? It's the night before the wedding!" But he was insistent; we should first finish counseling.

Billy wisely said, "Tom, no matter what is going on here, you are my pastor. You have been my friend for years. We are going to listen to you and wait."

And so hours before our scheduled marriage, we were calling friends and relatives and telling them of the change of plans. Actually, Billy did all the calling; I was too distressed. He even went to work with me the next day and explained to my fellow nurses why our plans had changed.

But what seemed like a dreadful problem actually worked for the good of both of us. I admired Billy's submissive spirit. Later Tom would respect Billy much more for his submission to authority. This trial truly did us no harm, and later I would be able to trust Billy more because of it.

On Tuesday, March 7, we finished with counseling. During this time our marriage license had expired. Billy visited me at work on Wednesday with an updated one. Billy made the arrangements with Tom Layman, and on Thursday, March 9, 1995, after a day's work, and with the mission residents as guests, we became Mr. and Mrs. William Schneider. "Til death us do part" was never more significant than at this marriage.

HIV has been a life sentence for us rather than a death sentence. We have the advantage of knowing that life is short, which makes us value each day in a way we might otherwise miss. The truth is, life is short and death a destination for all of us. We don't know any more than anyone else when it will be over. It has helped us to set aside differences and sift through what is really important. It encourages us not to carelessly waste our time on trivial issues. I have had much more fun in the present, and I am glad for that.

Having a few days off work, we discussed what do to. Billy said, "You know what I would like the best? I just want to go home." Home was going to be my house. Billy had been working there since his move, remodeling the kitchen and tearing up carpets, and already it felt like his as much as mine. So the Schneiders came home, and we felt at home with one another in spite of marriage on such short notice.

When I ask myself, "Why did I marry Billy Schneider?," the answer is obvious. It was God's plan. But what about love? Was this truly love at first sight? I don't think so. It was a combination of "zing" and faith at first sight. The love part came later. If it was God's plan, should we try to make everything fit, or would God take care of that?

My prayer was and continues to be that God will allow me to truly love my husband, and He answers that prayer every day. What once was impossible in my life happens daily. As a child who had been let down by every significant male in her life, for me to genuinely love a man is a miracle, and God has given us this miracle on top of all the others. This is true for Billy as well. He had no role models and no real experience for being a husband. In the last years of Linda's life, he became caretaker and did a wonderful job. Now his marriage is more of an equal relationship. In spite of the difficulties that such a relationship brings, God has allowed us to love each other even when things go wrong. We have fun together. There is rarely a night when we go to bed without having a good laugh about something silly. Yes, God is good. And yes, we are in love!

CHAPTER 24

Billy James

Many of you may be wonder what happened to "Edderic Patheteric." He had not been with us long when Billy began to allow him some freedom. He hated to see a dog chained, so Billy began letting him roam the yard with Midnight during the day. This seemed to work well as Midnight became a real watch dog, keeping Eddie away from the road. One evening Billy stood outside with the dogs, by now good friends, and said, "Eddie, do I need to chain you?" He decided against it, but in the morning Eddie was not with Midnight to say good-bye to me as I left for work. When I got to the end of the driveway, there was Eddie's lifeless body lying on the road. He had wandered into the street and been hit by a car.

We knew Eddie was prone to wander. He did not seem to sense the danger of the road. Billy felt so badly, so responsible for his death. Scooping him up from the road, Billy cradled his still warm body in his arms, and cried, "I'm sorry Eddie! I'm so sorry!" If only he had chained him the night before. And yet Billy knew that Eddie had strayed on his own. It was a difficult day for Billy as he felt the remorse, the guilt, of having left Eddie unprotected. To us it has been a picture of a dilemma we have had to face as we wrote this book. Responsibility – just whose is it?

Billy had been influenced very negatively by his environment. Alcohol use, physical abuse, and sexual abuse were a part of his childhood. But when he smoked his first cigarette at age twelve, who was responsible? And when he accepted his first shot of heroin, who was responsible?

Yes, Billy's life was affected by the sin of others. But he also is responsible for his own sin. He realizes that every day, knowing that he is HIV positive. He buried his wife Linda because of her drug use. His mother, her voice box gone and her lungs damaged by emphysema, is able to communicate only with the use of a machine because of cigarette smoking. And, of course, there is a long procession of his friends, buried because of their own drug use.

When does this change – from being sinned against to sinning oneself? From being influenced to being responsible? It is a difficult issue and one that Billy and I have wrestled with. We have begun to understand something about both the generational nature of sin and the personal nature of sin.

God's Word acknowledges that this is a difficult issue. Jesus, in Matthew 18 said, "Woe to the world because of the things that cause people to sin! Such things must come, but woe to the man through whom they come!" This verse seems to address both the generational problem of sin and the responsibility issue. Because of the sin of our common forefather Adam, we all inherit a sinful nature from our own parents. This makes it impossible to live without sinning against our own children and seems to be what Jesus is saying with the phrase, "such things must come." This passage is specifically dealing with the issue of abusing or sinning against children. Just prior to the verse, Jesus said, "But if anyone causes one of these little ones who believe in me to sin, it would be better for him to have a large millstone hung around his neck and to be drowned in the depths of the sea."

In spite of this inheritance, we all are responsible for our own sin. The Bible also is clear on this. "All have sinned..." (Romans 3:23, NIV)

Billy accepted responsibility for Edderic Patheteric when he accepted him as our dog. By not guarding him as he should have, he was responsible for Eddie's death. And yet, Eddie by himself had wandered into the street, which brings us to the need to write this chapter.

Billy's son, young Billy, has been mentioned only briefly. This is not his story, and yet he was affected by Billy's drug habit and therefore is an important part of Billy's story. Young Billy, whom we'll call "Billy James," surely is the product of his father's sinful nature, and beyond that, he was very much sinned against by his father. When Billy speaks to students, he sees Billy James' face in the faces in the crowd. Countless children and teens tell him stories that break his heart – stories of abuse by parents, of abandonment, of crimes committed against them.

Billy has recognized that the same is true of his own son, who has been missing for over four years. When Billy returned to his family as a new believer, Billy James accepted his Dad without a word of reproach. He never said to Billy, "Dad, where were you?" or "Dad, why did you take money from me for your drugs?" There were so many things Billy James could have said to his dad, but he did not. And yet, when Billy first spoke of his son's disappearance, his attitude was, "I'd like to get my hands on him! What does he think he's doing, abandoning his family in this way and breaking his grandmother's heart!" Billy was angry that his son had just disappeared.

But with the writing of this book, God has convicted the heart of another father about his son. God has been working on Billy Schneider, helping him to understand that he himself passed on a sinful nature to his son. And beyond that, he offended the boy and sinned against him. Because of his own addictions, he was responsible along with Billy James's mother for causing his unborn son to be addicted. Physically, Billy James received the drugs from his mother, but the influence of his father was an undeniable part of the picture.

Billy has seen the beauty in the attitude of the father of the Prodigal Son in Luke 15. The incredible part of this story is that if the father in this story is a picture of God the Father welcoming us at the moment of our salvation, then He is doing so without the need to recognize His own sinful nature. He simply does not have one. But as an example to us, what a way for an earthly father to welcome a wandering and wayward son! If parents would recognize that our children have sinned because of our sin, perhaps we could help them by taking responsibility as sinning fathers or mothers. What a homecoming it would be if Billy could welcome Billy James home by recognizing that not only did he pass on his own nature to his son, but he abused, he abandoned, he mistreated his son in his own addictions, forgetting and sacrificing everything, including his son, for the sake of the god of his body, drugs.

What would Billy say to Billy James if he could? "Billy James, I am sorry! I wronged you over and over. When you were a child, I put you into positions an adult could not handle. Oh, Billy James! No matter where you are or what you have done, I want to welcome you home! I want to shoulder the responsibility of my own sin, the sin which has affected every area of your life. Your father is a sinner, and he passed on his sinful nature to you. I want to hold you in my arms. I want to tell you I love you! Please come home!"

We recently have hired a private detective to search for Billy James. Much earlier, about six months after the disappearance, Billy asked his friend Jerry Carella to check the New York City morgue, looking for his son. He could not bear to do it himself. He thanked God that Billy James was not found there.

If only we could ask Billy James to speak. When his mother was sick, he began to withdraw from her, going to see her less and less in the hospital. Who knows what was going through the mind of an eighteen-year-old, whose mother was dying and whose father was HIV positive?

We have great hope for Billy James. Billy often has said, "God knows exactly where he is." And with that, Billy goes on. He cannot change the past. His past is in God's hands, and he is confident that Billy James is safe in God's hands as well.

When Billy and I were moving to South Carolina, we lost Midnight. The move was confusing – packing a truck, leaving that truck in Grand Rapids, Billy going to southern Michigan to speak and I to South Carolina to wrap up a job situation. Midnight was left in the hands of our good friend Steve. But Midnight obviously didn't get the picture right. He had no idea Billy was coming back for him. Feeling abandoned, he set off to find his family the moment the opportunity presented itself.

A long search ensued. Billy and I were both frantic, Billy because of the thought of losing Midnight, and I because I was sure I would lose both of them. How could Billy ever drive to South Carolina by himself, with all our earthly belongings in tow, knowing Midnight was gone? It was a black week in our lives. Billy was scheduled to leave Michigan on Monday. He called the Grand Rapids Press to put in a full page picture ad for his lost friend and companion. He was told that the Press did not do this for lost dogs. "However," said the lady on the phone, "I can give you a list of found dogs that came in over the weekend if you wish."

Desperate, Billy said, "Why not?" And the woman proceeded to give him an entire page of numbers to call. "Hopeless!" said Billy to himself. But with a prayer, he decided to try the first number on the list.

"Yes, we do have a dog. Now is your dog all black?"

"Well, yes, he is, except for a white star on his chest," replied Billy.

"Well, this dog has some gray or white along his hind legs," the gentleman on the other end replied. Suddenly Billy was not so sure of the description of his own beloved dog. "You are welcome to come and check him out," he was told. But as the conversation was coming to an end, Billy did not believe this could be Midnight.

"Wait a minute," said the finder of dog, "does your dog do something really strange in the bathroom?" And in that moment, Billy knew he had found Midnight! Yes, he does do something strange in the bathroom – he drinks from the toilet bowl. And if the lid were down he would try opening it, banging it up and down until someone got the hint. A thrilling reunion ensued.

We will never know what went through Midnight's mind as he roamed the streets of Grand Rapids or where he was actually heading. But five days later, he was found miles from Steve's house, and miles from anyone else. What we do know is that God had his eye on him and brought him home. We are confident that if God is that interested in a dog, He is much more interested in a human being. He will keep his eye on Billy James as well.

I believe God is waiting for a prophecy to come true: "He shall turn the heart of the fathers to the children, and the heart of the children to their fathers" (Malachi 4:6, NIV). The first part of this promise is happening. Billy's heart is turning toward his son. Now we pray the second part also will occur. Perhaps then a father/son reunion will be able to take place. We leave Billy James in God's hands until God sees fit to return him to us.

Meanwhile, Billy's ministry continues. Billy's aim is to share the gospel with everyone he comes in contact with. Billy is always witnessing. This means that our trips to the gas station, the grocery store, or wherever, may take much longer than the average trip. But who can become impatient when the gospel is being shared?

He and Paul Fleming have formed GOTeL Ministries, and they continue to speak in schools, in churches, and in prisons. "Lead me, Lord, I'll follow, anywhere you open up the door," is Billy's theme. Billy's anti-drug message is personal and powerful. His evangelistic message is equally powerful. If you don't walk the walk, don't talk the talk, someone has said. And Billy walks the walk. His message is worth hearing.

Epilogue

As this book is being completed, Billy and I are in the midst of dealing with a new challenge.

We'd been living in South Carolina for about a year and a half, launching a new ministry to drug addicts. Billy had opened a siding business, with the idea of teaching men a useful trade when they graduated from TLC. This did not work out as planned. God needed to show Billy that He had given him the gift to speak, to share his faith and convictions, but not to teach the finer points of being a siding mechanic.

In March, Billy traveled to Grand Rapids for several speaking engagements. He began experiencing abdominal pain, and, while I was at work in South Carolina, he underwent an emergency appendectomy in Grand Rapids. What a relief! Just his appendix! After nine years of knowing he was HIV positive, any symptoms were alarming. But leave it to Billy, I thought. And God!

God seemed to give me a message that very morning in Our Daily Bread, the devotional published by RBC Ministries. "Prepared for loss?" I had read. "We're never as prepared... as we think we are." Our relief was short-lived, and I began to reckon with the truth of those words when our friend and surgeon Bruce Bonnell called a few days later. "The appendix had a tumor in it. It has come back as non-Hodgkin's lymphoma." I thought Billy and I were as prepared as anyone could be for this kind of news. But when this news hit, we were no more prepared than anyone else.

We quickly decided that we needed to return to Michigan, the place we both looked upon as home. While we were preparing for this move, putting our house on the market, making a myriad of decisions, we had this thing, this enemy, staged. It's like sending out scouts in wartime, and there definitely was a war going on inside Billy's body.

At the same time, our beloved body of believers in South Carolina joined the ranks of prayer warriors on behalf of Billy's life. And across the country, others joined in as the news traveled. Three times, Billy has been anointed with oil, with petitions for his healing. Once, at our request, at our own church, and twice more in response to the desire of others who love Billy, and who believe in the healing power of prayer. We can imagine the commotion in heaven as prayer after prayer has gone up. One angel (or whoever the prayer messengers are) to another: "Another Schneider request! Just who is this guy, anyway, God?"

At first, tests began coming back negative – abdominal scan, brain scan, bone marrow (ouch!) tests. And then, about four weeks later, a chest scan showed massive tumor growth in the liver. Nothing there a few weeks ago! And the doctor said, "You stop everything you are doing and get to Michigan now."

So in the end, we left our home unsold, furniture and belongings partially packed, and got on a plane, headed for Michigan and a future unknown. This was an extremely rapid growing cancer, so much so that we could see growth along Billy's appendectomy scar.

We had more tough decisions to make. We had been offered many alternative approaches to cancer treatment. We decided not to just discard each of these, but check into them until we found something that put up flags for us. One remedy we felt had some merit was an herbal tea, and we immediately began using it. Billy dreaded the idea of chemotherapy, and thought perhaps he might avoid it by using the tea. But the oncologist said bluntly, "Without chemo you have about three weeks to live." So we combined herbal tea with chemotherapy. As an added insult to Billy's body, we realized it was time to begin the newer drugs for HIV as well. Billy had his first T-cell count in nine years, and the bad news was that it was 70. The good news also was that it was 70, not lower. We have heard of people whose count is zero.

We are learning to take each day as a gift. We are not projecting into the future with either good or bad days. But there is some good news. The chemo seems to have wiped out the obvious cancer cells. Our oncologist, Mike Zakam, by now our friend as well, says he feels the cancer is in remission. But he is cautious, saying there is no guarantee just when or how viciously the cancer could return. Meanwhile, we have more chemo treatments to deal with. And Billy is looking into marketing a whole new line of products, sure to take off like wildfire – "chemowheat" cereal and "chemoshave" (for the cleanest shave ever!) among them.

Also, Billy has had some wonderful family news. His mom was in the hospital for much of the winter, presumably near death. Billy was privileged to lead his mom to the Lord during this time. She has returned home and is doing better, although her health is fragile. We believe his Uncle Johnny is opening his heart to the Lord as well. He is not entirely sure what salvation is all about, but there is a definite change in this man whom Billy had not seen for eighteen years. One by one, Billy is seeing the lives of other family members change.

What is it that gives Billy hope and courage? What keeps him speaking when his voice is barely audible, as it is now? What keeps him sharing his faith? What makes him unafraid of death? What makes him desire that his life might be a model to others? It is Billy's life verse, Philippians 1:20. "I eagerly expect and hope that I will in no way be ashamed, but will have sufficient courage so that now as always Christ will be exalted in my body, whether by life or by death. NIV"

Billy and I covet your prayers. Remember, "the prayer of a righteous man (or woman or child) is powerful and effective" (James 5:16, NIV). If you do not know Jesus personally, we urge you, if you have been touched by what God has done for Billy, to make that decision for Christ now, as outlined on the next page. Don't think that you cannot pray. Remember Billy's wife, Linda, who prayed, as she said, when she didn't know the Lord. And her prayer was answered!

Billy and Joanne Schneider
1997

If you have been touched by the life changing love story between Billy and his Savior, perhaps the Holy Spirit is speaking to you about your own life. Are you tired of the direction in which your life is moving? Beginning a personal relationship with Jesus Christ is as simple as ABCD. Our prayer is that your life will be changed, as Billy's has been, by the incredible love of Jesus. Billy's relationship with Jesus has not meant an end to difficulties, but it has meant knowing someone who loves him is in charge. It does mean that with the difficulties comes a peace that "passes understanding," and it has given him direction and purpose in his life.

A - ACCEPT that you're a sinner. Romans 3:23 - "All have sinned, and fall short of the glory of God." Romans 6:23 - "The wages of sin is death."

B - BELIEVE that Jesus bled and died for you. Romans 6:23 - "...the gift of God is eternal life in Christ Jesus our Lord." Romans 5:8 - "God demonstrates his own love for us in this: while we were still sinners, Christ died for us."

C - CONFESS that Jesus is Lord. Romans 10:9,10,11 & 13 - "If you confess with your mouth 'Jesus is Lord,' and believe in your heart that God raised him from the dead, you will be saved. For it is with your heart that you believe and are justified, and it is with your mouth that you confess and are saved. Anyone who trusts in him will never be put to shame. For, everyone who calls on the name of the Lord will be saved."

D - DECIDE who you're going to live for. Romans 12:1,2 - Therefore, I urge you...in view of God's mercy, to offer your bodies as living sacrifices, holy and pleasing to God. Do not conform any longer to the pattern of this world, but be transformed by the renewing of your mind."

If you would like to begin a personal relationship with Jesus Christ (be "saved"), and you accept that you're a sinner, this can be done by way of a simple prayer (talking to God, either aloud or in your heart.) An example of such a prayer is: "Dear God, I know that I have sinned against you. I need a savior. I understand that you have offered your Son Jesus Christ as this savior. I believe that He bled and died for my sins. I believe that Jesus is Lord. Thank you for your gift of eternal life "

If you have prayed this prayer, or similar one, we would be interested in knowing.

Billy & Jeanne

Mail the attached card to let us know of your decision.

Name_____

Address_____

City_____ State_____ Zip____

I prayed to recieve Christ as my Savior on (date)_____

I would like a Bible_____

I would like prayer for_____
_____

BUSINESS REPLY MAIL

FIRST CLASS MAIL   PERMIT NO. 446   MUSKEGON, MICHIGAN

POSTAGE WILL BE PAID BY ADDRESSEE

Gospel Films, Inc.
PO BOX 455
MUSKEGON MI 49443-9969

NO POSTAGE
NECESSARY
IF MAILED IN THE
UNITED STATES